THE CREATION AND
DESTRUCTION
OF VALUE

THE CREATION AND DESTRUCTION OF VALUE

The Globalization Cycle

Harold James

HARVARD UNIVERSITY PRESS
Cambridge, Massachusetts, and London, England
2009

Library of Congress Cataloging-in-Publication Data

James, Harold, 1956–

The creation and destruction of value : the globalization cycle /
Harold James.

p. cm.

Includes bibliographical references and index.

ISBN 978-0-674-03584-3 (cloth : alk. paper)

1. Globalization—Economic aspects.   2. Financial crises.

3. International economic relations.   I. Title.

HF1359.J357   2009

337—dc22   2009015221

To Knut Borchardt

CONTENTS

ACKNOWLEDGMENTS

I should like to thank Michael Aronson of Harvard University Press, who inspired this book and expertly guided it through publication. I have given some parts of the book as lectures or in seminar discussions at a number of institutions, and am profoundly grateful for the interesting discussions that ensued. In particular I should like to thank President Yves Mény at the European University Institute; President Günter Stock and Stephan Leibfried of the Berlin-Brandenburgische Akademie der Wissenschaften; Gyan Prakash and Jan Plamper at the Davis Center at Princeton University; Paola Subacchi at Chatham House; James Hoge at the Council on Foreign Relations; Harvey Sicherman at the Foreign Policy Research Institute; Eric Helleiner at CIGI, Waterloo, Ontario; Jonathan Kirshner at Cornell University; Marc Flandreau at Sciences Po; Heinz Herrmann at the Deutsche Bundesbank; Daniel Posner at the UCLA International Institute; Mark Spoerer at the Humboldt University, Berlin; David Marsh and the German-British Forum; Manfred Pohl and Marnie Giuranna at the European Association of Banking History; and Hartmut Berghoff at the German Historical Institute in Washington, D.C. Luis Tellez at the Witherspoon Institute has given constant support and encouragement and generated a stimulating intellectual atmosphere. Both Princeton University and the European University Institute have provided ideal conditions for working. I am very grateful for research funding from Princeton University and from the European Union's Marie Curie Program, grant MEXC-CT-2005-024362. I have also had very helpful suggestions from Knut Borchardt, Michael Bordo, James Boughton, the late Gerald Feldman, John Ikenberry, Christopher Kobrak, and Ashok Mody. Brooke Fitzgerald, Raymond Hicks, David Mills, and David Schaengold gave me invaluable assistance with the preparation of the manuscript and the figures. Julie Carlson guided the copyediting in an exemplary way.

Finally I express my deep appreciation of Marzenna James, as well as of Maximilian, Marie-Louise, and Montagu James, who have always wanted to hear more about the financial crisis.

INTRODUCTION

TEN YEARS AGO, I began writing a book on the phenomenon of globalization. In part it was an attempt to understand the bitter debate pitting globalization protesters against international institutions that attempted to manage the inherently chaotic process of increased flows of goods, capital, and labor. How permanent and how stable was globalization?

The wave of often violent protests reached a height in riots at the World Trade Organization (WTO) meeting in Seattle in 1999, and at the G-7 meeting in Genoa in 2001. The annual meetings of the World Bank and the International Monetary Fund (IMF), and of the private-sector World Economic Forum, also provided the backdrop for all kinds of militant action. There was an escalation of rhetoric, as the mayor of London, Ken Livingstone, in 2000 demonstrated his lack of either historical sense or responsibility by proclaiming that the IMF and the World Bank had killed more people than had Adolf Hitler.[1]

But it was hard for the protesters to decide who was the real villain, or against whom they should be struggling. Very often they instead chose symbolic protests, targeting branches of McDonald's or Starbucks. There was a real catalyst for these clashes, the fallout from the severe East Asian financial crisis of 1997–1998, but few of the antiglobalization activists entertained constructive plans to deal with the problems of worldwide poverty. Yet even without such a strategy, during the early years of the twenty-first century the world seemed calmer, and the world economy grew quickly, spreading economic growth across more countries, creating new opportunities, and helping to alleviate a great deal of poverty.

The book that resulted from my reflections ten years ago, also published by Harvard University Press, suggested that globalization was reversible, and that indeed in the interwar period the Great Depression had finally ended the sustained era of globalization that had begun in the second half of the nineteenth century with the advent of the steamship and trans-atlantic cable. But it also suggested that the antiglobalization protest movement had no binding ideology that was capable of creating a new model of order that could supplant globalization, one analogous to that envisaged by the antisystem movements on the left and right, by communists and fascists, in the interwar era.[2]

Ten years later, there is an obvious urgency about the crisis. The complaint against global institutions is not that they are too strong or too interventionist, that they detract from national sovereignty, but that they are ineffective. Protesters have a much clearer sense of who is the enemy. One organizer of the action against the 2009 G-20 summit meeting in London, an academic anthropologist, told a BBC news program, "We are going to be hanging a lot of people like Fred the Shred [the sobriquet of the banker who had brought the Royal Bank of Scotland to catastrophe] from lampposts on April Fool's Day and I can only say let's hope they are just effigies."[3] The radical struggle against globalization had become much more clearly a fight against global capitalism. And it had become clear to everyone that at least one version of global capitalism, that driven by financial innovation, was profoundly flawed. The question of what replaces the vision of globalization, then, today compels a more immediate solution.

The major difference between 1999 in Seattle and 2009 in London at the G-20 summit was not, however, the character of the protest. It lay in a shift in power. In Seattle, there was no doubt that the most powerful person was the President of the United States, Bill Clinton, and that he was influenced and moved by the fervor of the protesters. In London, the President of the United States, Barack Obama, was calm and distinguished. But his was the assured distinction of a man who is responding with dignity to the coming of a new order. He was taking a leaf out of the history of how Britain managed its long story of decline and marginalization. Other national leaders lived up to national stereotypes. Nicolas Sarkozy produced a spray of brilliant ideas. Silvio Berlusconi hugged presidents Dmitry Medvedev and Obama like a Latin lover. Angela Merkel spoke movingly about a new opportunity of creating "capitalism with a conscience," with all the moral earnestness of a modern German who is also the daughter of a Lutheran pastor. Gordon Brown had an impressive command of detail but looked rather dour. None of these figures was really central to the formulation of a response to global crisis. Who would have predicted at earlier moments, in 1989 when communism collapsed in central Europe or in 1999 when the United States could lay out its idea of a moral order, that the most powerful figure in a meeting on the future of capitalism would be a communist official? China's president, Hu Jintao, was powerful not simply because of the rapid growth of the Chinese economy since the 1980s, but also because China had emerged as the major provider of global savings and global surpluses. He made it clear that China would assert its own interests, whether on the question of Tibetan independence or on the character of the international currency regime. He held in his hands the future of globalization. But these recent shifts in power within our global institutions, as well as in how we understand these interactions, are fraught with peril.

One of the reassuring mantras of the past decades has been that globalization—the integration of the world through large flows of goods, capital, and people—is irreversible. Until very recently, modern people took comfort in the idea that, although the Great Depression ended what might be thought of as an earlier episode of integration, the depression era was unique and held no real lessons for the present. The breakdown was produced by such an odd confluence of causes as to be incapable of repetition: the legacy of the First World War and of the financial settlement of reparations and war debt; the chaotic and ill-regulated banking system of the largest economy of the world, the United States; and governmental inexperience in handling monetary policy in a world that was still pining for metallic money. Yet historians have often said that this reasoning about the nonrecurrence of profound structural breaks may be quite wrong. In fact, there is nothing inexorable—or new—about globalization.

By contrast, an overwhelming majority of modern economists were misled by treating short-term trends as if they were permanent phenomena that could be used to derive reliable behavioral correlations and extrapolations. There were some exceptions, notably among the followers of Hyman Minsky, and some economists, notably at the Bank for International Settlements, who were concerned with credit bubbles; but such analysts were dismissed as alarmist or eccentric, not only by the commercially driven economists who worked for financial institutions as de facto salesmen, but also by the overwhelming majority of academic economists, who were also subject to commercial pressures in the forms of peer evaluation and patterns of career development. These economists instilled a false complacency in politicians and other policymakers.

This book offers reflections on the phenomenon of globalization and its cyclical propensity to generate backlashes and collapses. In particular, it suggests that:

1. The phenomenon of globalization has today become a ubiquitous way of understanding the world, but people who used the concept as a tool of analysis failed to understand its volatility and instability.

2. Globalization not only involves international movements of goods, people, and capital, but is also associated with transfers of ideas and shifts of technology, which affect and restructure our preferences.

3. In consequence, globalization generates continuous uncertainty about values, both in a monetary and a more fundamental (nonmonetary) sense. It is much more than an economic phenomenon.

4. Globalization is vulnerable to periodic financial catastrophes, which involve very sudden alterations of concepts of value. That is, our values themselves are reevaluated during such crises.

5. During a crisis, unexpected and apparently random linkages become apparent. People begin to see in what complex ways the world has become interconnected.

6. A major focus of the reevaluation of values involves worries about radical monetary instabil-

ity, sometimes about deflation (collapsing prices), sometimes about inflation (rapidly rising prices), but often schizophrenically about both phenomena at the same time.

7. The perception of instability calls into question the sophisticated techniques devised for monetary management, whether through the complex operation of the international gold standard in the nineteenth-century globalization and during its brief and abortive interwar revival, or via the paper (fiat) currencies of the post-1970s world.

8. In the uncertainty of globalization setbacks, the experience of the past becomes a powerful template for understanding the contemporary predicament. People refer back to past crises, and historians come to be prophets. Today, we look back to the Great Depression of the late 1920s and 1930s as a model for what can go wrong when globalization breaks apart.

9. Politics and economics are inextricably and inherently linked, and politics provides an alternative to market mechanisms for the management of globalization crises.

10. When breakdowns occur, reconstruction is extremely difficult and involves a long and ardu-

ous effort for the rebuilding of social trust.

Value renewal takes time.

Some time ago, the English historian J. H. Plumb wrote about the very sudden emergence of political stability in early eighteenth-century Britain, which he treated as a big surprise with astonishingly long-lived consequences.[4] But the restoration of a structure of values is rarely that simple. It takes new initiatives of imagination and innovation.

In this book, I first examine the tortured discussion of contemporary globalization, then consider breakdowns of the interwar period. It is puzzling that for a long time, historical attention was focused on 1929, an economic and financial crisis that had obvious policy solutions, rather than on 1931, an upheaval for which it is harder to find easy answers. Here I relate the story of the economic and ensuing geopolitical vulnerability of recent decades, before turning to the question of how values are reevaluated.

1

THE END OF GLOBALIZATION:
A MILLENNIAL PERSPECTIVE

GLOBALIZATION IS NOT only a process that occurs somewhere out there—in an objective and measurable world of trade and money. It also happens in our minds, and that part of globalization is often more difficult to manage. To understand both the process and our reactions to it, we need a historical grounding.

Describing the very dynamic global trade of the second half of the nineteenth century and the early twentieth century has become part of the repertoire of economic historians.[1] But that era was not the only episode of globalization.[2] Archaeological evidence indicates that trade had a global reach during the Roman empire, with Roman coins being traded in coastal regions of Sri Lanka and Vietnam. There were subsequent expansions of global trade and finance. In many of them, ideas from classical antiquity and from the Roman age of globalization (and global rule) were revived, as in the economic rebound of the late fifteenth and early sixteenth centuries (the economic backdrop to the Renaissance), or the eighteenth century, during which improved technology and increased ease of communications opened the way to global empires (for Britain and France).

All of these previous globalization episodes ended, almost always with wars that were accompanied by highly disruptive and contagious financial crises. Globalization is often thought to produce a universalization of peace, since only in a peaceful world can trade and an interchange of ideas really flourish. But in practice, a globalization of goods, capital, and people often leads to a globalization of violence.

It is thus possible to speak of globalization cycles, with long periods of increased interchange of goods, and flows of people and capital. But then something happens. People feel there has been too much interaction; they draw back from the global setting and look instead for protected areas in which they can be safe from global threats and global devastation. The shock or trauma is often connected with financial collapse, especially the profound uncertainty that financial disaster brings. At each stage in the globalization cycle, we tend to extrapolate and to think that this particular phase will last forever: whether it is the confident upswing, or the stagnation and anger of the downward movement of the cycle. A break in the upward trend thus produces profound disorientation and disillusionment.

By the end of the twentieth century and the beginning of the new millennium, after decades of expanding trade, and in the aftermath of the collapse of the state-planned alternative of communism, many people had come to the conclusion that globalization was an irrevocable and irreversible fact. When my book *The End of Globalization* appeared in 2001, some reviewers felt that even to suggest the possibility of a new reversal of globalization was to be unrealistically pessimistic.[3] Others thought that a book that showed the vulnerability of globalization must necessarily be an antiglobalization screed.

DEBATES ABOUT GLOBALIZATION

The globalization optimists had existed in earlier eras. In the early nineteenth century, the euphoric liberal globalizers John Bright and Richard Cobden were convinced that enhanced commerce would engender peace and stability, and they spread their message with evangelical fervor. A similar case was made just before the First World War by Norman Angell.

There were only a few dissident voices, such as John Henry Newman's criticism of Bright or Cobden's attempts at "expedients to arrest fierce wilful human nature in its onward course, and bring it into subjection": "ten years ago [that is, 1854, before the outbreak of the Crimean War] there was a hope that wars would cease for ever, under the influence of commercial enterprise and the reign of the useful and fine arts; but will anyone venture to say that there is any thing any where on this earth, which will afford a fulcrum to us, whereby to keep the earth from moving onwards?"[4]

In the 1990s, globalization was hotly contested, with some authors making the argument about inevitability or its unstoppable quality, and others bitterly opposed to a development that they saw as a new version of imperialism. Opponents, however, often found it hard to develop an alternative that went beyond a backward utopia of returning to national economies and domestic production, or a forward utopia of global citizenship. The idealists in particular liked to protest against the "inevitability" of globalization.[5]

After the millennium, however, something very peculiar happened to the globalization debate. The ferocious ideological discussions that accompanied the protests against the Seattle WTO meeting or the Genoa G-7 summit faded, replaced by a generalized sense of gloom. The massive demonstrations that disrupted the 1999 WTO meetings, or the 2001 Genoa summit, or the annual meetings of the World Bank and the IMF or of the Davos World Economic Forum—which took place in a generally expansive and buoyant world economy of the new millennium—seemed to belong to a distant and rather innocent past. Perhaps some of the new appreciation of globalization came as previous antiglobalizers began to see that they might themselves take up causes and values that transcend national frontiers, and in that way might themselves become globalizers.[6]

But in large part, the older antiglobalization sentiments were outflanked by a much more radical antiglobalization. The new realism came from the awareness that Islamic fundamentalism cut across the distinctions among antiglobalism, anticolonialism, and globalism: it rested on a genuinely global vision in which godliness could recognize no territorial frontiers, and should make no compromise with corrupt and degenerate states. Modern capitalism was much less the enemy than was the particularism of existing state structures. After the terrorist attacks on New York and Washington on September 11, 2001, the authentic voice of antiglobalization was now promoting a very different global vision.

Many of the former critics now saw at least some advantages of globalization. The more intelligent insisted that they always wanted a "better globalization," rather than simply wanting to turn back the clock.[7] In particular, the dramatic growth of India and China seemed to demonstrate that opening to the world market is a way not only of producing growth but also of alleviating poverty.[8] Most Third World activists wanted more, not less, globalization, and a dismantling of the trade barriers of the industrial countries. They now complained that there had not been enough of the right kind of globalization.

CRISES AND GLOBALIZATION

Part of the new sobriety of the 2000s depended on an understanding of how globalization until that point had entailed not smooth development ever upward and onward, but repeated crises. In part this more realistic and less euphoric vision of the costs of globalization derived from analyses of the upheavals in the nineteenth-century era of globalization.[9] But it also came from contemporary experience of crises that often served a cathartic purpose, pushing countries to adopt policy reforms that led to greater openness and market liberalization, and that potentially could prevent recurrence. Indeed the story of the collapse of communism and central planning could be interpreted as an extreme version of such a transformative crisis. It was those countries in the 1980s most exposed to Western capital markets, Poland and Hungary, that found themselves in the greatest economic difficulty and thus had the most urgent need to reform. The Soviet Union, which only started to borrow on a big scale in the second half of the 1980s, rapidly found itself in the same sort of crisis, from which radical reform appeared the only appropriate exit strategy. Crisis is thus fundamentally built into the structure and functioning of a globalized economy.

The integrated world economy has been shaken by repeated crises—stock exchange upsets, debt crises, Mexico's "tequila effect," the "Asian flu," contagion in Russia and South America. The dramas have led to more and more unease about "globalization"—or alternately, as its critics call the process, "neoliberalism," "turbo-capitalism," "casino capitalism," "disordered capitalism," "capitalism pure," or "Anglo-Saxon economics." With every crisis, an initial reaction is that the new events spell the end of a particular model of liberal economics, the so-called Washington consensus. In fact, although some crises can be cathartic and push policymakers to take corrective measures, others can be Carthaginian. In the history of the past two centuries there has only been one such radically destructive crisis, the Great Depression, and it is not surprising that we are terrified of repeating the experience.

More recent crises have alternated between storms in the periphery and blowouts at the financial center. The 1980s Latin American crisis was followed by a decade of American stock market and housing booms that eventually collapsed. The emerging market and largely East Asian crisis of 1997–1998 was followed by a similar bubble in the United States, and after 2007 by a terrifying meltdown emanating from the United States. Most recently, national governments and international agencies have been overcome with paralysis.

What are the consequences of the periodic collapses? Will the party resume again, or is the newest and most serious episode a step on the road to a profound backlash against globalization and integration? In 1997–1998, the U.S. government and international financial institutions had held up the American system as a model for emulation. One decade later, the roles seem to be reversed, and it is Asia that now has the right to lecture the Americans, while Europeans are confidently predicting the imminent export of a European social model to the United States. There is a new level of radical uncertainty about institutional design.

Analyzing what went wrong is the key to learning from the cathartic crisis, as well as to preventing the Carthaginian one.

Despite the shocks and shrieks of the 1980s and 1990s, there was no real interruption. On the contrary, the drive to the market became faster. Even former critics became converted into proselytes. Experiments in heterodoxy were ever shorter-lived. While the Mitterrand government experimented for two whole years between 1981 and 1983 with a French alternative to Reaganomics and Thatcherism, a similar experiment in a new ideology of demand management lasted only five months in Germany in 1998–1999 with the brief tenure of Oskar Lafontaine as a radical socialist finance minister. The slogan of the new age, which was much ridiculed at the time, became that associated with Margaret Thatcher: TINA (There Is No Alternative).

In most countries, old political divisions between right and left no longer made sense in the light of globalization. At the heart of the left-right divide had been a struggle for redistribution, with the left wanting to redistribute more, and the right wanting less redistribution. In democracies, this often produced a convergence around the center, in that both left- and right-wing parties needed to appeal to a median voter. This seemed to rule out either extreme of expropriation or the absence of redistributive taxation. In the last decades of the twentieth century, however, the factors of production became more mobile. Small countries such as Sweden with deep social democratic traditions had to lower their rates of corporate taxation in order to prevent an exodus of firms. Instead of a left-right divide, a new center emerged that welcomed globalization. In Latin America, leftists with a Marxist background saw international openness as a way of modernizing society.[10] So did the Communist party in some parts of India, notably West Bengal; and so, above all, did the Chinese Communist party.

There was thus more convergence and consensus about the idea of the market economy than at any previous time in the twentieth century. A joint paper by German chancellor Gerhard Schröder and British prime minister Tony Blair in 1999, "The Way Forward for Europe's Social Democrats," set out the new politics of what they called a "new middle." It was strongly market oriented: "The weaknesses of markets have been overstated and their strengths underestimated." It pleaded for an economic deregulation and liberalization that had to a great extent already taken place in the United Kingdom, but not in Germany: "Product, capital, and labour markets must all be flexible." And it admitted that the old left-right dichotomy no longer made much sense. "Most people have long since abandoned the world view represented by the dogmas of left and right. Social democrats must be able to speak to those people."[11] These new-style social democrats drove forward a process of liberalization and deliberately light regulatory intervention. When Tony Blair's eventual successor, Gordon Brown, was chancellor of the Exchequer, he pressed forward with a strategy of "regulation lite" for financial markets that promised to make London once more the world's preeminent financial center.

One response to the power and the global commitment of the new political center was the emergence or strengthening of radical parties on the political extremes, who collected protest votes against the "system." Both right and left protested against internationalization and globalization, and its bureaucratized institutions, the IMF (for emerging countries) and the EU (for rich European countries). There were some powerful voices on the right who tried to raise national issues and national myths as a challenge to globalization, and who attracted cross-national attention (and usually disapprobation): Patrick Buchanan in the United States, and in Europe, Jean-Marie Le Pen, Jörg Haider, Christoph Blocher, the German "Republican" movement, and Italy's Northern League. The left rejectionists, by contrast, found it hard to mobilize behind charisma, and tended to form fractious and fissiparous parties.

Instead of concentrating on the battle for redistribution, which had been the political theme of the world after the Great Depression as well as after the Second World War, societies in the East and West looked for new political issues—in part because when capital flows undermined the capacity and the efficacy of national redistributionist politics, old-style politicians looked helpless. Politicians instead focused on the environment, on corruption, in short on issues not simply or directly related to an agenda of redistribution. They felt their voters had become convinced of the hopelessness of conventional politics, which seemed to offer no real choice.

THE PSYCHOLOGY OF GLOBALIZATION

Some of the hardest obstacles to globalization are not economic, but rather lie in the domain of social psychology. It is here that a sense of helplessness is profoundly pervasive. We find it hard psychologically to deal with the consequences of global openness. Europeans who often still ride in trains divided into compartments, as opposed to the open cars of traditional American railroad transportation, often encounter a routine variant of this difficulty. Someone getting on the train and entering a compartment is treated with suspicion. There is an atavistic reaction against the intruder who wants to take space away. But as the traveler settles in, at the next station he becomes part of the "in" group, and it is the new outsiders getting onto the train who are treated with suspicion. Christianity instructs its adherents to "love thy neighbor as thyself," with the implication that the neighbor is different from people farther off, with whom there is no social interaction. But the dynamic character of globalization means that a vast quantity of trivial and long-distance interactions are created, and neighborhood becomes impossible. Indeed many modern city and suburban dwellers know their neighbors much less well than people living far away. The German sociologist Ulrich Beck recently wrote that "what unites people everywhere, not just in Europe but all over the globe, is a longing for a world that is just a little less compulsorily integrated."[12]

Each major modern crisis has produced arguments that a new Great Depression, and with it a collapse of globalization, is possible, or perhaps even likely. As yet, it has not happened. The most direct risks emanate from the financial system, and from the possibility of contagious financial collapse in a well-integrated world. What made the Great Depression "great" was a series of contagious financial crises in the summer of 1931, and the subsequent trade response. But the protectionist policies that followed built on a backlash against globalization that had been developing progressively since the last third of the nineteenth century. That backlash identified globalism with negative change or even sin, and held that moral regeneration required national cultures.

THE ROBUSTNESS OF GLOBALIZATION

By 2005 and 2006, by contrast, globalization seemed to be extraordinarily robust. It apparently easily survived the shock of the terrorist attacks of September 11. There was no repeat of the contagious emerging market crises of 1997–1998, and some people even thought that the IMF as a crisis manager would inevitably go out of business. Initially, the credit market anxieties of 2007 produced little echo in Asian emerging markets, with the result that many commentators began to speak of a "decoupling."[13] This resilience of the world economy was then erroneously interpreted as a demonstration of the inexorable character of globalization.

In fact globalization's history is full of surprises. These startling turns in modern economic history, all of which led in the direction of a more open and a more connected world, are worth considering in the current context.

The first surprise concerns the opening of trade. It can be read as a suspense drama, with a new twist to the narrative on almost every page. The General Agreement on Tariffs and Trade (GATT), formed in 1947, was a compromise. It achieved its biggest successes in the 1960s, largely at the cost of reducing its reach so as to exclude some of the most contentious trade items—textiles and agricultural products. By the 1970s, after the collapse of the Bretton Woods par value system, most writers agreed that the GATT was moribund. The Tokyo round of 1973-1979 was protracted and spotty. In the mid-1980s, the leading experts concluded that the GATT was "in a state of breakdown." The ministerial meeting of 1982 had failed. The Uruguay round of 1986-1993 looked doomed to failure as the United States and the European Community became locked in a politically complex struggle over agricultural pricing and subsidies. Even in 1993, on the eve of the final agreement of this round, a major text produced by a GATT official had as its theme "the weakening of a multilateral approach to trade relations," "the creeping demise of GATT," and the fact that "the GATT's decline results from the accumulated actions of governments."[14]

But then came the astonishing extension of multilateral principles to intellectual property and trade-related investment, as well as the creation of a more complete conflict-resolution procedure and the institutionalization of multilateralism in the World Trade Organization. At that time, commentators were skeptically insisting that the United States would ignore the new institution and instead continue a unilateral exercise of power through application of the discriminatory clauses of Super 301 of the 1988 Trade Act. But when the first ruling came against the United States, the United States accepted it. In 1998, everyone gave reasons why an agreement on financial services could not be realized. Then, apparently unpredictably, at the last moment it came about. The WTO negotiations went on into the Doha round, which was repeatedly declared dead, but nevertheless managed repeated resurrections.

The second startling development, which had accompanied the trade revolution, was the liberalization of capital movements. At the time of the 1944 Bretton Woods Conference, almost every economist believed that volatile capital markets—hot money—had been the mechanism of contagion through which the Great Depression had spread internationally. They felt it was highly unlikely that international capital flows would resume quickly. The bankers had seen their credits frozen and their reputations attacked, and the badly burned fingers of the bondholders were still clutching the defaulted and worthless paper issued by governments all over the world. But even if capital movements did by some unlikely chance resume, the thinking at Bretton Woods was that there should be international and national policy instruments available to control them. The 1944 Bretton Woods agreements required the liberalization of payments for goods and services, but there was no equivalent demand to free movements of capital, and the new institutional arrangement assumed that capital movements would be permanently restricted. In fact, however, it was very hard for governments to put such limitations on capital. Offshore markets developed, and eventually, in the early 1970s, large flows of money brought down the Bretton Woods regime. Even so, many capital controls remained in force, and impeded capital flows. It was only recently that the consensus view embracing trade liberalization was extended to the capital account; and even then, such a demand was not included in the IMF's Articles of Agreement.

Capital flows remained very volatile; and indeed each crisis brought fresh calls—even ingenious schemes—to reintroduce some measure of control, or to discriminate between useful and speculative, destructive movements. After the great crises of 1992–1993 in the European Monetary System (EMS), there were demands for some way to slow down the process, or to give the directing forces of the state greater traction. The Mexican peso crisis of 1994–1995 produced the verdict that the situation was not a consequence of human error, but rather of "the collapse of an economic model." In 1997, Malaysian prime minister Mahathir Mohamad blamed international speculators and the hedge funds for economic turbulence. He was not alone. The influential and Nobel Prize-winning economist Joseph Stiglitz wrote that by pursuing not a global good but "the interests and ideology of the Western financial community," the IMF had intensified the crisis and caused economic hardship, as well as political destabilization with riots and governmental collapses.[15]

Labor flows constituted the most controlled part of the international economy during the recent experience of globalization. In the classical Industrial Revolution, before 1914, people had moved relatively freely, although from the 1880s the United States attempted to control Asian immigration. Immigration is the area most vulnerable to the protectionist impulse. This was where in the 1920s a decisive backlash against internationalism occurred, one accompanied by the hardening of unpleasant and also short-sighted nationalistic arguments.

Immigration is a sensitive political issue, often coupled in popular debates with the "globalization" theme. Indeed the arguments on this issue are ancient: both Aristotle and Aquinas recognized that some products needed to be traded over long distances, but believed that local production was more moral, because foreigners would disrupt civic life.[16] In every major economy except Japan, the number of foreign-born workers has been rising since the 1980s. In the European Union before the eastern enlargements of 2005 and 2007, there were over 20 million legal immigrants, and an estimated 3 million illegal aliens. An official study, jointly produced by Mexico and the United States, suggested that there were just over 7 million Mexican-born people living in the United States, of whom almost 5 million were legal residents at the turn of the millennium. Illegal immigration has increased with an uptick in mass travel, the removal of bureaucratic restrictions, and the end of communism.[17] Many governments tacitly accepted that—apart from periodic amnesties and legalizations—there was no real way of controlling the flood of illegal workers who moved into poorly paid grey-market jobs.

In the early 1990s, a number of academic studies showed a comparatively limited impact of trade on labor income.[18] The results were so reassuring that the issue largely died away as a topic for debate. Ten years later, when economists began to revisit the theme and suggested that a wider range of jobs might be "offshored," globalization appeared so firm that little could be done. The most dramatic effects of globalization were seen in the market for unskilled labor, and consequently most policy thinkers simply saw better training as an answer. More recently, however, it has become clear that skilled service jobs (most conspicuously in computer software but also in medical and legal analysis) can also be "outsourced" or "offshored."[19] Consequently, the gigantic Western middle class—the great winner of the twentieth century—is now extremely alarmed by the prospect that it might be overtaken by an even larger (and harder working) middle class in emerging market countries, especially because it is contending at the same time with a large and widening gulf between its potential for acquiring wealth and that already achieved by a new global elite.

The middle class has often been particularly vulnerable to crisis. The very rich have sophisticated wealth management and hedging techniques, and may be able to move their assets internationally; and the very poor have little to lose. Between these groups, middle classes have a strong sense of their possessions, and react with anger to losses.[20] The story of interwar Europe, where the middle classes turned en masse to the radical right, offers a terrifying case study.

The middle classes and their fears were at the center of the political campaigns of both U.S. presidential candidates in the crisis year 2008. The successful French presidential candidate of 2007, Nicolas Sarkozy, spoke of a "revolt of the popular and middle classes who reject a globalization that they consider not as a promise but as a threat."[21] The political backlash drives an intense populist concern in the rich industrial countries with corporate governance, corporate abuses, and the excesses of executive pay.

One other tack was taken by some proponents of the antiglobalization case. They suggested that globalization might bring increases in material welfare, but that, according to strong empirical evidence from psychology, this increased income did not produce long-lasting improvements in happiness or well-being. Increased consumption might bring a short-lived emotional high, but without more continually repeated consumption, the high could not last. If I buy a beautiful new car, I will be impressed by its technical performance and sophistication—but only for a while. I will soon yearn for a car that is even faster and more complicated and luxurious. There is, in other words, a continuous ratchet effect, because we compare our position to what we were some time ago. Robert Frank referred to this phenomenon as "luxury fever."[22] His examples are predictably American: the rising demand for super luxury goods that have unnecessary features that are never employed: the high-performance SUVs that are really only used in slow-moving suburban traffic, or the high-performance, restaurant-quality kitchens that are installed in homes whose owners hardly ever cook. Depending on your sensibilities, such observations will amuse or shock you.

The modern theoreticians of happiness go on to make a policy recommendation on the basis of these observations. Since the urge to consume involves wasteful demands as a way of asserting positional superiority in a world in which there is still considerable scarcity, a higher tax regime would redistribute goods without in any way reducing either efficiency or happiness. Luxury fever is, in fact, according to the economist Richard Layard, an addiction that can be usefully taxed as a form of deterrence in the same way as we agree that cigarettes, alcohol, sugared beverages, and even (in some countries) coffee should be taxed.[23] Taxation is a way of ending the rat race. So a rational world that takes happiness maximization as its goal would have a high rather than low tax regime. The new economics of happiness has, in other words, become the major rationale for high rates of taxation after the collapse of other types of justification. Governments have taken it up, as in the 2002 document produced by the British Cabinet Office on "life satisfaction."[24]

Anti-immigrant or antitrade sentiment alone has not fueled the newer version of the globalization debate. The most pervasive feature of the new world is a sense of helplessness, produced by altered expectations about what politics can do. Our angst is in large measure so intense because of the way in which the lopsided internationalization (more for capital than for labor) has decisively limited governments' ability to act. Although there is no "eclipse of the state," the traditional role of states is challenged by globalization.[25] Taxes on capital are limited by the possibility of "exit" (in Albert Hirschman's terminology) resulting from the new mobility of the factors of production (and especially of capital). The result is an alteration of the political game, and a reduction in the space for political self-assertion and for privileged elites.

By contrast, the first Industrial Revolution was accompanied by an expansion of the state. New wealth gave greater resources to governments, and new problems called for collective solutions. By the late nineteenth century, a German economist, Adolph Wagner, even formulated a "law" of the constant growth of state expenditure, and of the increasing share of national income devoted to the state. The organization of the new states, bureaucratic and hierarchical, was mirrored in business organization, with numerous layers of authority and control.

Governmental growth in the twentieth century was fueled by military expenditure. After the Second World War, there was no retrenchment of the public sector. On the contrary, the expansion of the state continued at a faster rate in the recovery years after the Second World War, and persisted even in the poor economic circumstances of the 1970s.[26] Dani Rodrik has pointed out the character of the bargain made during the great period of postwar trade expansion: those states that opened themselves most to trade (small European states such as Austria, Denmark, the Netherlands, Sweden, as well as Germany) also embarked on higher state spending on income transfers, in order to create a safety net that would catch the disruptive social fallout of the open trading economy.[27]

The consequence of state-generated security systems was to make globalization look more stable. The world economy was also performing with apparently both more efficiency and more equity than ever before. Indeed, the global economy of the millennium looked extraordinarily resilient and dynamic. Real (price-adjusted) growth in the world economy increased in the 1990s from 3.5 to over 4 percent, and further gains occurred in the 2000s.

While the enhanced role of government may have provided for more stability, the dynamism of the global economy came from a very different source. The better growth performance was a result of financial globalization.[28] Financially driven globalization offered a new technology—which was in keeping with the fact that in almost every case, the movement to globalize is also associated with dramatic technical innovation. This new form of globalization had the capacity to ensure a more efficient allocation of resources and thus to raise the long-term level of growth on a world level. Its late twentieth-century effects were most visible and most dramatic in emerging market economies. Those countries became the dynamos driving international economic growth. But then something went profoundly wrong with the course of financial globalization.

2

WHICH HISTORICAL ANALOGY
APPLIES, 1929 OR 1931?

WHENEVER PEOPLE want to understand apparently inexplicable events, they look to a historical parallel. Two iconic dates, 1929 and 1931, are usually cited in the context of the contemporary crisis. References to both these dates, but especially to 1929, increased in frequency during the financial crisis of 2007–2009, most markedly after the dramatic worsening of the crisis in September 2008. In absolute terms, there were many more references to 1929, though as I will argue in this chapter, it is wrong to identify 1929 with the Great Depression.

Both 1929 and 1931 played an important part in the story of the final collapse of the first twentieth-century version of globalization. But they mean completely different things. The year 1929 marked an American stock market collapse, while 1931 was characterized by a worldwide contagion in which banks fell like a row of dominos.

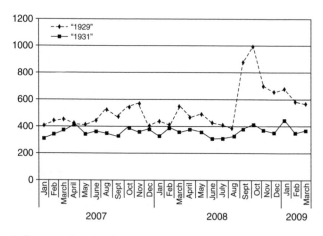

References to "1929" and "1931" in major newspapers, 2007–
2009.

Source: Lexis-Nexis word search.

The term "1929," then, stands for the irrationality
of financial markets. The interplay of millions of independent decisions is radically indeterminate, producing outcomes that no rational observer could
predict. As a consequence, the stock market crash of
October 1929 remains a historical puzzle, with no
economic historian having been able to provide a
completely satisfactory and convincing explanation.
The crash was largely a U.S. phenomenon, and the di-

rect ramifications for the rest of the world were not immediately visible.

By contrast, "1931" refers to the profound vulnerability of financial systems. Banks are inherently vulnerable institutions, in that they transform term structures—in other words, they convert short-term deposits into long-term credits. They expect that in the normal course of events not all depositors will want their money back at the same time, and the demand for particular withdrawals will follow from motives that are not correlated with those of other depositors. Even if the term structures are not altered by the bank, many bank borrowers do not expect to have to repay the bank abruptly. As a consequence, when some big simultaneous shock occurs, or when a financial institution is threatened by insolvency, or even when there is no way of knowing whether there is a threat but there is a general climate of uncertainty, there may be coordinated withdrawals of deposits. But the banks cannot repay all their creditors at once. If they try, they may force their debtors into bankruptcy.[1]

During the nineteenth century, especially in the United States, bank runs were regular occurrences. In the course of the twentieth century, governments and central banks began to realize that some measure of regulation and supervision could make generalized fear of a banking panic less likely. Part of the reassurance was the promise that all depositors or all creditors are treated equally. But globalization and financial connectedness mean that banks lend across jurisdictional boundaries. New sets of motives come into play: a government may, for instance, have an interest in having its banks in effect expropriate the assets of foreign but not domestic creditors. Such calculations are especially likely to be made in economic downturns, when debate focuses around how sacrifices should be distributed. It is always politically tempting to find some way to make the foreigner (that is, the nonvoter) pay the costs and assume the burdens.

The 1931 crisis was an obvious accident waiting to happen. It stemmed from a fundamental fragility of the institutions of banking, especially when faced with a deflationary spiral. In its immediate consequences, it was much more severe than 1929. A series of contagious banking and currency crises brought down one central European country after another. The chronology begins with the apparently unique case of the Austrian Creditanstalt, which collapsed on May 11, 1931. The panic then spread to Hungary, and more significantly to Germany, where the collapse of the Darmstädter Bank on July 13, 1931, in turn precipitated a crisis in Great Britain and forced Britain off the gold standard on September 21, 1931. Speculation turned against the United States, had a desperately destructive effect on U.S. banking, and only stopped in April 1933 when, under the new regime of Franklin Roosevelt, the United States also left the gold standard. In a sad and prolonged aftermath of the Great Depression, the remaining gold-standard countries, notably Belgium, France, the Netherlands, and Switzerland, continued to be buffeted by financial panic until in September 1936 the so-called Gold Bloc finally disintegrated.

The two sorts of crises required different types of policy responses. Situations like 1929 could and can be dealt with by the provision of increased liquidity, and by the conventional tools of monetary policy. Responding to 1931-style events, by contrast, is institutionally more complex, and requires the reconstruction of whole banking systems. The complexity increases when there is a high degree of external indebtedness denominated in foreign currencies, and when the restructuring of the entire financial sector

requires the alteration of many microeconomic institutions. In the historical setting of the original
"1931," enhanced banking supervision and regulation
were required, as were deposit insurance, the split-
ting of the system into different types of banking
(as in the United States under the terms of the Glass-
Steagall Act), and new measures for bank recapitalization. These measures were implemented between 1933 and 1935. In the long run, they produced
greater stability, but they did not result in immediate
economic stimuli in the way that liquidity enhancement or fiscal activism does in response to a 1929-
style crisis. In other words, there is no simple macroeconomic formula for dealing with this second sort
of financial disturbance, in which the microeconom-
ics of finance are profoundly disturbed. After a "1931,"
it is impossible simply to wave a magic wand and return the world to stability.

In a "1929" situation, then, policy is tested by the
need to respond to a particular problem, but there
are answers. In a "1931" crisis, it is much harder
to find policy failures, because crucial errors were
made long before the crisis even broke out. This is
one reason that, some time ago, the German economic historian Knut Borchardt warned against a

"retrospective optimism about the solubility of problems."[2]

The two types of crisis seemed to be localized differently, especially insofar as public opinion and pol-
icy-relevant memory are concerned. The 1929 event is
largely thought of as a very American experience, although of course there were large stock-exchange declines in all countries during the Great Depression.
And though there were thousands of bank collapses
in the United States during the Great Depression, almost all the institutions concerned were small (because of the fragmented character of U.S. banking).
The failure of really big institutions that immediately
set off a domino response looked like a peculiarity of
the central European situation.

The geographic difference contributed to the very
distinct political responses to these various forms of
financial malaise. In the end, it is even possible to tell
an upbeat story about 1929 that includes recovery after tremendous setbacks, or "singing in the rain." By
contrast, "1931," which proved far more detrimental
to globalization, is a tale of central European angst,
and of powerful and destructive longings, urges, and
actions. The European crisis of 1931 actually spread
the European malaise to the American continent,

and transformed a rather ordinary economic downturn into the Great Depression.

1929 AS A MODEL

The U.S. stock market crash of October 1929 is indisputably history's most famous financial collapse. It is evoked wherever and whenever financial sentiment becomes nervous. Policy recommendations for the following eighty years have consistently been made on the basis of analyses or presumptions of what went wrong in 1929.

In particular, John Maynard Keynes's *General Theory of Employment, Interest, and Money* (1936) has at the heart of its diagnosis a critique not of the general operation of the stock exchange but specifically of the American market and its peculiar experience: its propensity to encourage a destabilizing and irrational speculation, which followed from the obsession of market participants with psychological rather than economic dynamics and expectations. The problem for Keynes lay fundamentally in a system of valuation in which values had no necessary or direct correspondence to long-term productivity. As a result, the American market became a casino with an inherently destabilizing quality. It was uniquely volatile because of the extent of popular participation, while more exclusive or "aristocratic" markets were less vulnerable.

> A conventional valuation which is established as the outcome of the mass psychology of a large number of ignorant individuals is liable to change violently as the result of a sudden fluctuation of opinion due to factors which do not really make much difference to the prospective yield; since there will be no strong roots of conviction to hold it steady. . . . The actual, private object of the most skilled investment today is "to beat the gun," as the Americans so well express it, to outwit the crowd, and to pass the bad, or depreciating, half-crown to the other fellow. . . . Even outside the field of finance, Americans are apt to be unduly interested in discovering what average opinion believes average opinion to be; and this national weakness finds its nemesis in the stock market.[3]

Extreme financial turmoil was, in other words, a specifically American malaise.

Keynes's analysis became the most influential policy prescription for the middle of the twentieth century: it required government action (on fiscal policy) to stabilize overall expectations and in this way establish a predictable or, as Keynes would have called it, "conventional" framework for the valuation of economic activity, and thus for the functioning of a market economy. In the 1960s, President Johnson's advisers repeatedly justified the combination of tax cuts and expansion of social spending as necessary in order to avoid a repetition of the 1929 disaster. In the mid-1970s, in the aftermath of stagnation and the first oil-price shock, the world again relearned a Keynesian lesson from the experience of the Great Depression.

In 1987 a seemingly exact replication of the stock market panic led to a different lesson, but again one historically derived: that a massive liquidity injection was needed to stop a stock market crash from becoming a generalized business depression, because of the danger of a destabilization of financial institutions and of credit intermediation. This was the monetarist or Friedmanite conclusion. Again, like Keynes's analysis, it was derived from a very detailed historical study of what Milton Friedman and Anna Schwartz in their monumental *Monetary History of the United States* termed the "Great Contraction."[4] Their emphasis was on how a stable monetary framework created the sole basis on which expectations could be reliably and predictably formulated. Their interpretation played down the significance of the October 1929 panic, and explained the Great Depression in terms of the Federal Reserve's mistaken policy after 1930 of not reacting to bank failures, which produced a colossal monetary contraction (deflation).[5] The 1929 crisis has, in short, become a standard part of the justification offered both by central banks for stabilizing monetary policy and by governments for stabilizing fiscal policy.

More recently, the volatility of financial markets has increased due to the globalization of markets. The memory of 1929 is now used with each financial crisis (whatever the origin), as part of a call for stabilization policies and for a fundamental rethinking or reversal of financial liberalization. Helmut Schmidt, for instance, who as German chancellor in the 1970s had been obsessed by the possibility of another Great Depression, in 1997 after the East Asia crisis stated, "The main parallel lies in the helplessness of many governments, which had not noticed in time that they had been locked in a financial trap, and now have no idea of how they might escape."[6] The financier George Soros at the same time warned of "the imminent disintegration of the global capitalist system," which would "succumb to its defects."[7] The aftermath of the 2007 subprime crisis has produced similar reactions. Again, George Soros opined, "This is not a normal crisis but the end of an era."[8] The chairman of the Swiss bank UBS, while defending himself from criticism about his own and his institution's particular failings after an $18 billion writedown, noted that the world was experiencing the "most difficult financial circumstances since 1929."[9] The statement is typical of market sentiment during bad times, but is also curiously erroneous. Most of the world, and particularly European countries, still had considerable financial stability in 1929; the really severe jolt, the *annus terribilis,* came in 1931. There are also other perplexing misapprehensions: the bad day on Wall Street is often called "Black Friday" although the dramatic market falls were on Thursday, October 24, 1929, and Monday and Tuesday, October 28 and 29.

THE MYSTERY OF 1929

The 1929 crisis is a substantial curiosity in that it was a major event, with truly world-historical consequences (the Great Depression, even perhaps the Second World War), but no obvious causes. Above all, the supposed causes can only be very poorly fitted (if at all) into the still prevailing paradigm of social science explanations in the "efficient markets hypothesis." According to the "efficient markets" view, stock prices accurately reflect all the publicly available information about a security; they will not change without the availability of new information.[10] Panics in which prices change very abruptly cannot easily be conceptualized in terms of this hypothesis, especially if there appears to be little in the way of new information driving the panic. In consequence, financial crises have become a major rhetorical resource for critics of efficient markets.[11]

Belief in the nonrationality of 1929 is closely correlated with skepticism about the operation of markets. There exists a continued fascination with 1929, and with books that tell its story, notably Frederick Lewis Allen's *Only Yesterday,* John Kenneth Galbraith's *The Great Crash,* John Brooks's *Once in Golconda,* and Charles Kindleberger's *Manias, Panics, and Crashes* (with Kindleberger's work alone offering a broader perspective than just 1929).[12] All are frequently republished, and seem to be widely consulted as guides to contemporary financial panics. It might be plausible to think that this is one area where historical study has had a really formative influence on the behavior of a very large number of market participants.

Significantly, around 1929 there were equivalent financial disasters in other large industrial countries, which in each case contributed to a worsening of economic fundamentals and to the severity of the Great Depression. In April 1927 Japan was shaken by a series of bank panics after the Bank of Taiwan suspended operations. Germany was brought down by the failure on July 13, 1931, of the Darmstädter und Nationalbank. Britain was pushed off the gold standard on September 21, 1931. But in each case, it is possible to give a relatively clear account of what caused the panic. The Japanese failures were the result of a political controversy over the "earthquake bills" held by the Bank of Taiwan that had been given special treatment after the disaster of the 1923 Great Kanto Earthquake. The German banking crisis followed from a coincidence of a political crisis following the announcement of the Austro-German customs union and the difficulties of a major textile producer, Nordwolle. Britain was propelled into a crisis by a deep split within the government over fiscal policy and unemployment benefits, as well as by an unprecedented naval mutiny that nervous commentators saw as the beginning of a British Bolshevik revolution.

The unique feature of the American panic is that no one has ever been able to explain convincingly what caused it, or even what the specific trigger for the panic might have been. There are two potential "rational" explanations, but they are not very satisfying.

One is that investors were able somehow to guess that there would be a Great Depression.[13] There were certainly some signs of slowing in the U.S. economy, and construction had peaked several years before, in 1926, and fell off (in part perhaps because of declining flows of immigrants). But there was no evidence of a general downturn. There exist no direct measures of consumer confidence for the early twentieth century, but until the last quarter of 1930, when there was a distinct change of tone, most surveys of business confidence were relatively upbeat. Periodicals such as *Business Week* were discussing an upturn in the summer of 1930. Peter Temin has identified as the most significant business indicator the change of classifications by bond rating agencies (Moody's, and Standard and Poor's), and shown that in 1929 and even in 1930 a smaller proportion of corporate bonds were downgraded than in 1921 or 1937.[14] In other words, there is no hard evidence that anyone in 1929 could or should have expected a significant fall in American output or employment. In any case, if 1929 is treated as a cause of the Great Depression, there is no reason to believe that the depression was an obvious "fact" in October 1929: there is an obvious circular quality to that kind of explanation. There is a much stronger case that 1929 led to the Great Depression because of policy errors in the management of a stock market panic.

Perhaps, however, people experienced in political economy foresaw the likely effects of a big policy mistake, the tariff bill that became known as Smoot-Hawley.[15] The bill had its origins as an election promise of Herbert Hoover's in October 1928 to address the plight of the farming population. During congressional debate, first in committee and then in the full House, large numbers of nonagricultural tariffs were added, so that the eventual act included some 21,000 tariff items. Over the course of October 1929, the likelihood that Congress would pass the bill increased significantly. Financial prophets might have pondered the possible or likely forms of trade retaliation by other countries. But there is no real sign of such discussion of the probable path of world trade.

Nevertheless, the consequences of the new tariff may have been reflected in some market responses, and the immediate outside price signal given to the financial markets on October 24 was a sharp fall in some commodity prices.[16]

The inability to find a precise cause of the 1929 panic is baffling and intriguing. Paul Krugman once asked: "Could a small cause have large effects? Yes, it could. After all, the Great Depression had no obvious cause at all."[17] Ben Bernanke put the point even more vigorously, stating that "to understand the Great Depression is the Holy Grail of macroeconomics."[18] Social scientists (and maybe also policymakers) are thus in an endless quest for causes. Is it—like searching for the Grail—fundamentally a futile pursuit? Were those affected by the Great Depression simply buffeted by wildly unpredictable psychic upheavals?

THE DEVELOPMENT OF STOCK PRICES

Just as twentieth-century financial markets worried about a repeat of 1929 at the first sign of a downturn, market participants in 1929 were obsessed with the possibility that the panic of 1907 would recur. The dramatic collapse in October 1907 had been preceded by a sustained expansion, and a vigorous merger and acquisition movement, with a steady rise in stock prices that convinced many small-time investors that they should enter the market. As an indication of the extent of the collapse, the Dow Jones Industrial Average, which had risen from 49.90 at the beginning of the century to a high of 75.45 in January 1906, fell to a low of 38.83 on November 14, 1907. The impact was not long-lived: after a short and deep depression in 1907–1908 there was some recovery. But the old speculative fever did not return, and the index was still only just over 50 in 1914, when hostilities broke out in the First World War.

Between early 1926 and the spring of 1929, the Dow Jones Industrial Average index almost doubled, from 158.54 at the beginning of 1926 to 308.85 at the end of March 1929; then it moved ahead even faster during the summer, with a peak of 386.1 on September 3. The rise was a response to loose monetary policy, and produced a euphoria that led many people to believe that the boom would go on forever.

The first signs of weakness in the market appeared on September 3, but small falls tempted many new investors into the market, so that volatility and trading quantities rose. On September 20, in England, the conglomerate built up by Clarence Hatry collapsed, and the New York market responded with a 2.14 percent fall. During the week of October 14, the fall in stock prices accelerated, with dramatic drops on October 16 (3.20 percent), October 18 (2.51 percent), and October 19 (2.83 percent), though they were punctuated by a 1.70 percent rise on October 17. But the first day of real panic was Thursday, October 24, when the market fell very abruptly from an opening of 305.85 to a low of 272.32. Major New York bankers assembled at the offices of J. P. Morgan, as they had on a famous occasion in the panic of 1907, and a senior Morgan banker, Thomas W. Lamont, told the press that "due to a technical condition of the market," there "had been a little distress selling on the Stock Exchange."[19] The public outcome of the meeting was that the vice president of the New York Stock Exchange, Richard Whitney, whose brother was a Morgan partner, went onto the floor of the exchange and made a series of bids aimed at stabilizing the market. The first of these, a bid of 205 for 10,000 shares of U.S. Steel, became one of the central collective memories of the New York market. The market indeed went up again, although in the afternoon selling orders from across the country continued to stream in, and the Dow Jones Industrial Average Index closed at 299.47, in other words down only 2.09 percent on the day. The daily volume of share transactions, which earlier in the year had been in the one to two million range, was 12,895,000.

An initial press comment for Thursday, October 24, emphasized the irrationality of imagination. The *New York Times* noted: "At the climax of such a movement, the speculative imagination runs as wild as it does on the crest of an excited rise. Whereas it pictured impossible achievement in prosperity and dividends last August and last February, it now looks for equally impossible disasters."[20] Impossible? Not for long.

Over the weekend, there was a brief pause for reflection, as commentators commented and moralizers moralized. The result was an even more extreme panic on the following Monday (October 28), which continued on the Tuesday, with very high trading volumes (9,213,000 and 16,410,000 shares, respectively), and declines of the Dow Jones Industrial Average by 12.82 percent on the Monday and 11.73 percent on the Tuesday.

On Monday, there was no repeat of Richard Whitney's appearance and of the stabilizing bid for U.S. Steel. Instead, rumors about the continued bankers' meetings suggested that they had agreed to a con-

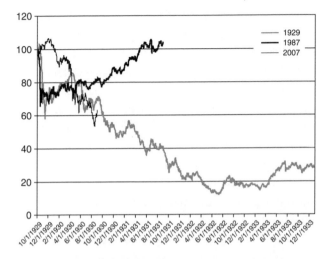

Stock price movements, 1929–1933: percentage change in the Dow Jones Industrial Average, with comparable developments from October 1987 and October 2007. October 1929/1987/ 2007 = 100.

Source: Global Financial Data.

certed *selling* of stock, and Thomas Lamont was obliged to issue a formal rebuttal. In fact, New York banks did dramatically increase their lending to brokers at a time when out-of-town banks were calling in loans, and foreign institutions were undertaking massive withdrawals.

On Wednesday, October 30, there was a dramatic bounce, with a gain of 12.34 percent and again, exceptionally high trading volumes (10,727,000 shares); Thursday, too, had a gain of over 5 percent. After that, however, bad news continued. On November 2, the failure was announced of the Foshay utilities company of Minneapolis, which owned companies in twelve states. Again, the weekend was filled with rumors that the bankers' committee was liquidating stocks. The market slid until, on November 13, the Dow Jones Industrial Average closed at 198.69. This slump was followed by a spectacular (but incomplete) recovery to 294.07 on April 17, 1930. After this, there was a long slide, with fewer bounces, until the trough of July 1932, with a low of 40.56 occurring on July 8.

The selloff of October 1929 was exacerbated by interruptions to communications caused by the extent of the panic. Phone lines were swamped not only by an unprecedented volume of calls, but also because escaping steam at 120 Broadway happened to put phones out of action. Lines between New York and Boston, Montreal, Chicago, Detroit, Cleveland, and Toledo were overwhelmed; the transatlantic phone lines had twice their normal business.[21] The sheer volume of orders meant that some were simply overlooked, even though clerical workers continued to process orders until after midnight; downtown restaurants remained open, with every table occupied until early in the morning.

In the longer term, policy failures also exacerbated the impact of the stock market crisis. The first reaction of the New York banks had been to replace the credits that had been called by out-of-town banks, but this left them with an increasing vulnerability as lenders worried about the quality of loans. The Federal Reserve Bank of New York immediately stepped in to provide liquidity to the market by open market operations (purchases of government securities) that increased bank liquidity; and the Federal Reserve System also bought securities during the last three months of 1929. But New York's operations had not been approved by the Washington Board or its Open Market Investment Committee, and they became the subject of increasing criticism in Washington. The board eventually succeeded in suspending the New York actions.

Why did the Washington federal institutions behave in this damaging way? The board's actions were based on the erroneous theory that it had the responsibility to respond to the needs of the economy by discounting bills, but only "sound" bills that related to actual physical sales of goods, not to financial or speculative transactions. This "real bills doctrine" produced catastrophic monetary destabilizations in the early twentieth century: inflation in Germany and central Europe, where the central banks insisted that they were just responding to an exceptional but real business demand; and deflation generally in the early 1930s, in which real transactions simply seemed to dry up and the central banks in a symmetrical way reacted to what they thought was declining output.

Some explanations go further, and suggest that the U.S. central bank was gripped by the liquidationist doctrine that was memorably formulated by Treasury Secretary Andrew Mellon: "liquidate labor, liquidate stocks, liquidate the farmers, liquidate real estate. . . . purge the rottenness out of the system."[22] This was certainly the view of some influential thinkers of the time, who saw, as did the British economist Lionel Robbins, the problems of the 1920s as lying in an inflationary overextension of credit.[23] The idea of purging the ills out of the system, which was at the heart of the outlook of Robbins, as well as of Mellon and the Federal Reserve policymakers, depended on an extensive moral and psychological theory of what had gone wrong with the American economy.

THE MACROECONOMIC EFFECTS OF
THE STOCK MARKET CRASH

From 1929 to 1932, U.S. gross domestic product (GDP) fell by a third, from $103.1 billion to $58.0 billion. The dramatic quality of this collapse has never been matched in the postwar era, where very slight recessions were followed by quick recoveries.

How much of the collapse was the result of the precipitous drop in the stock market? The Dow reached its low of 40.56 points in July 1932. Investors (sometimes described as 600,000 widows and orphans) lost more than $20 billion as a result of the stock exchange collapse, and consequently reduced their consumption.[24] This is a vast amount of wealth, but it still does not account for the extent of the drop in GDP. In a detailed investigation, Peter Temin showed how at the beginning of the slide into depression in 1930, only $1.3 billion of the $3 billion drop in consumption could be explained by the panic.[25]

Another factor was probably more important. The reduced wealth as a consequence of the stock market panic reduced the collateral on which individuals and corporations could borrow, and thus pushed the process of credit disintermediation that charac-

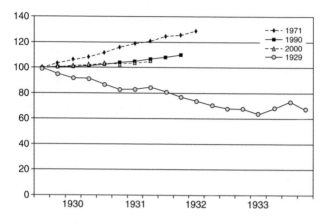

Index of real GDP in response to depression and recession.

Sources: For 1930s, Nathan S. Balke and Robert J. Gordon, "Historical Data," in Robert J. Gordon, ed., *The American Business Cycle: Continuity and Change* (Chicago: University of Chicago Press, 1986), pp. 794–795; for postwar recessions, Bureau of Economic Analysis.

terized the Great Depression.[26] The effects of wealth reduction were thus magnified and augmented through their impact on the structure of credit.

Clearly, the Great Depression was the result of more than one chain of causation, and other independent influences made the crisis more intense and spread it across national boundaries, making it hard to isolate the effects of the drop in stock prices. Such autonomous causes included the long slide in commodity prices since the mid-1920s; the political disputes over war reparations and debts between the wartime Allies; the beggar-thy-neighbor trade policy that ricocheted across the world after the Smoot-

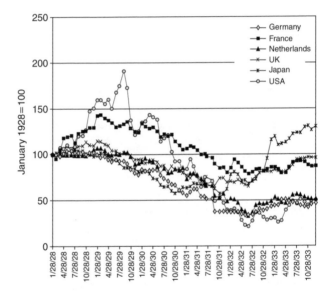

International stock indices in the era of the Great Depression. January 1928 = 100.

Source: Global Financial Data.

Hawley tariff; and the fixed-exchange-rate regime of the international gold standard, which proved to be a ready mechanism for the transmission of monetary deflation from one country to another. But of course, in one sense, all these provided information that might be expected to influence the multitude of market participants buying and particularly selling on the stock exchange.

It is striking how October 1929 did not lead to dramatic panics on other stock markets in Europe or Asia, where the news from Wall Street was just one more element in an increasingly gloomy economic picture. In a world of very substantial capital mobility, it is surprising how disconnected the different stock markets were and how these markets treated October 1929 as a U.S. phenomenon.

THE EFFECTS OF THE PANIC ON WELL-BEING

A great deal of the early fascination with the stock market crisis focused on its psychological effects. Newspaper comments immediately picked up on suicides as a result of the market, such as that of John G. Schwitzgebel of Kansas City, who had shot himself in the chest at the Kansas City Club on October 29. Crowds formed expecting to see distraught investors and brokers jumping from the Wall Street skyscrapers. Every popular history of 1929 picks up this focus. J. K. Galbraith recounts how "two men jumped hand-in-hand from a high window in the Ritz. They had a joint account." But he goes on to show that there were actually fewer suicides nationwide in October and November than in the summer months, when the market "was doing beautifully."[27]

The press also reported incidents of heart attacks, such as that suffered by David Korn while watching the stock ticker in his broker's office in Providence.[28] It is easy to imagine how exposure to intense stress and fear would be reflected in temporarily increased blood pressure. Research published in 2008 has tried to link coronary disease and bank failures in a more rigorous and systematic way. A study at Cambridge University used historical data to show how a systemwide financial crisis increases deaths from heart disease by an average of 6.4 percent in wealthy nations and by more in developing countries. The leading author of the survey, David Stickler, told the press, "Our findings show that financial crises aren't just about money—they also impact on people's health. This report shows that containing hysteria and preventing widespread panic is important not only to stop these incidents leading to a systemic bank crisis but also to prevent potentially thousands of heart disease deaths."[29]

In this regard, there is a significant difference between financial and political crises. The unhealthy effects of financial crisis do not usually appear in moments of political stress. In fact, political upheavals may indicate increased levels of hope about a better future. The result is a general decrease in levels of mortality related to physical stress and distress: thus in Poland in the Solidarność crisis of 1980–1981, deaths from heart disease and cancers (as well as from violence) fell, as they did in 1989–1990 when the communist system collapsed.[30] In each case, a plausible working assumption is that political turmoil was accompanied by a sense of optimism and of the possibility of change for the better. By contrast, the rise in fatal cases of heart disease and of cancers in New York City during the Great Depression is much more striking than the much more commented on suicide statistics, with deaths from heart disease per 100,000 rising from 257.4 in 1928 to 264.9 in 1929 and then to 275.5 in 1932 (and falling from 1933). It is clear that the financial panic was accompanied by a rise in physiological stress, which was a reaction to the sense that the future consisted literally and psychically of loss and renunciation.

INTERPRETING THE CRASH

The newspapers on October 24 emphasized simply the abnormality of the market responses over the past days, especially the Monday and the Wednesday, with their massive trade volumes: "It was very manifest on both occasions, to experienced Wall Street watchers, that the market was not acting as it had usually done when causes of special weakness had been eliminated."[31]

A striking feature of the reporting of the crisis was how much reference was made to the past history of crises as the only guide to current experience. The day after the October 24 collapse, the *New York Times* carried on page three an article entitled "Breaks of the Past Recalled on Street": "Many reminiscent comparisons were made yesterday with other periods of critical readjustment on the stock market. It was generally agreed that no previous decline this year and in 1928 compared in either scope or violence with the break of this month. . . . Comparisons most frequently made by older members of the Stock Exchange yesterday were with 1920, 1907 (the 'panic years'), 1903 and 1901."[32] In other words, history was the major reason why individuals suddenly felt that there might be a broad range of alternative, much lower, valuations of stock. History actually induced the sense of crisis. But it was a deep history, in that it lay outside the actual experience of the vast majority of market participants.

Exactly the same historical parallels, but this time to 1929, have been the stock-in-trade of commentary in every subsequent stock market panic. The most obvious parallel to October 1929 was the global stock market collapse of October 1987, with very similar percentage declines (22.61 percent in the Dow Jones on October 19), though a significantly different outcome: no world Great Depression of the interwar type followed. Again, market weakness during the preceding week was followed by a weekend replete with doom-laden journalistic prophecies. Again, as in 1929, there was no obvious trigger or news item, with the possible exception of the news that the United States had attacked an Iranian oil station (announced in the early morning of October 19). In the event, there was no world war, but there was a world panic.

In the immediate aftermath of the October 1987 crash, surveys of individual investors and of institutional agents were conducted to attempt to judge whether their motivation could be explained principally by reference to economic fundamentals, or rather to an endogenous determination because of some psychological theory of panic based on historical comparisons. On the basis of surveys, Robert Shiller concluded: "Investors had expectations before the 1987 crash that something like a 1929 crash was a possibility, and comparisons with 1929 were an integral part of the phenomenon. It would be wrong to think that the crash could be understood without reference to the expectations engendered by this historical comparison. In a sense many people were playing out an event again that they knew well."[33] The historical reference is in other words a continuous and necessary driver of financial crises: in euphoric states, people are prepared to imagine futures that they can paint in utopian terms; when the euphoria collapses, they pick up memories of past disasters (that they may never have personally witnessed).

One repeated point made very early in commentaries on the panic was that there were historical precedents to the speculative boom. The past experience seems to contradict the repeated claims made during the period of market euphoria that there existed some entirely novel phenomenon that transformed business relations and hence was likely to bring a permanent prosperity. The following report, from 1929, is thus a perfectly characteristic postcrisis diagnosis, with its strong dependence on historical reminiscence. "Indeed, the favorite principle that times have so far changed that nothing of pre-war finance could nowadays be repeated, ignored rather singularly the fact that all these eccentric notions were recurrently in absolute control of the speculative Wall Street mind as far back as 1901. They were dispelled and discarded then, as they have been on the present occasion, through contradiction of all of them by the emphatic action of the stock market itself."[34] Looking back into a distant past was the way of remembering the giddy heights that had been reached and of searching for a new sobriety. This was indeed how the increasingly common but erroneous recall of "Black Friday" came about: it was a reference to the collapse of (Friday) September 24, 1869, that was conflated with (Thursday) October 24, 1929.

In this regard, reassurances from experts or authorities were irrelevant or counterproductive. Government officials—from the President down—as well as financial institutions emphasized that the markets were fundamentally healthy. In a radio address on October 29, 1929, the assistant secretary of commerce reminded his audience that President Hoover had said that the "fundamental business of the country is sound." There were again echoes of this in 1987, when President Reagan shouted to reporters, "There is nothing wrong with the economy . . . all the business indices are up. Maybe some people see a chance to grab a profit."[35] In 2008, President Bush tried to be similarly reassuring, to no avail, and in 2009 President Obama reflected that stocks might represent a good value.

Big private-sector players also thought they had an obligation not only to talk the market up, but also to put their money behind their assurances. In 1929, John D. Rockefeller broke a long public silence to issue a statement: "Believing that fundamental conditions of the country are sound . . . my son and I have for some days been purchasing sound common stock."[36] Similarly, in 2008–2009, Warren Buffett made big stock purchases as a demonstration of his essential confidence.

On October 30, with further falls in the market, the leading stockbrokers all went out of their way to reassure their clients. Hornblower & Weeks announced that "yesterday's amazing volume would seem to indicate that the process of liquidation was in its final stages." Jackson Bros., Boesl & Co. concluded that "yesterday's record-breaking market" meant "that forced selling had been practically completed and that the stock market had touched its natural bottom." Clucas & Co. was more modest: "We do not expect an immediate turn in the market for quick profits, but do believe that purchase of sound securities around current levels will prove a profitable investment over a period of time."[37]

While the experts tried in vain to sound reassuring, a different sort of opinion was articulated with increasing fervor. Moralistic commentators from outside the financial world attributed the crisis to the wages of sin. The *New York Times* extensively reported Protestant—though not Catholic or Jewish—responses to the stock market turmoil. The Bishop of Winchester (England) was by coincidence preaching on the Sunday after the Thursday crash at Grace Protestant Episcopal Church on Broadway. "Whatever this financial crisis in Wall Street means, it means distress to many innocent persons. But I shall not be sorry it has come if it has administered a severe blow to that gambling spirit which attempts to get something for nothing, to obtain large profits at the ruin of others." The Reverend Trowbridge of All Angels Episcopal Church tried to express some sympathy: "Though I do not believe it is morally or economically sound to gamble as men and women have been doing with ever increasing fervor, and though I cannot help but feel that they have in a sense received their just deserts, nevertheless one feels desperately sorry that they should have to suffer such humiliation and defeat." The Reverend Overlander of St. John's Evangelical Lutheran Church on Christopher Street called for a more philosophical approach: "True, a lot of money was involved and in some cases, I suppose, some men and women were literally wiped out. Yet I wonder how many of those persons stopped to think, even with that hard blow, how many things they should be thankful for."[38]

The governor of New York, Franklin D. Roosevelt, criticized the "fever of speculation."[39] When in 1933 Germany defaulted on its international debt, he slapped his thigh and said that it "served the bankers right." His Treasury secretary, Henry Morgenthau, later explained his vision of the Bretton Woods agreements as driving "the usurious money lenders from the temple of international finance." This tone spilled over into the general interpretation of the character of the crisis. Keynes, whose background in the philosophical school of G. E. Moore and in prewar Bloomsbury made him unlikely to think in theological terms, concluded in *The General Theory* that "the sins of the London stock exchange are less than those of Wall Street."[40]

The Great Depression was also accompanied by inquiries and court cases aimed at punishing the evil-doers. Starting in April 1932, Ferdinand Pecora, chief counsel to the Senate Committee on Banking and Currency, pushed the committee into an examination of the bankers' actions. The chief executive of Chase, Albert Wiggin, was attacked for short-selling the stock of his own bank during the panic of 1929. Charles E. Mitchell, the chief executive of National City Bank, in March 1933 was arrested for tax evasion on share deals. Richard Whitney, the temporary hero of October 24, 1929, was arrested and imprisoned. The punishment of individuals seemed a good way of purging the system of a legacy of policy mistakes when it was hard to ascertain the underlying or fundamental causes of the market panic.

1931

The 1929 crash has no obvious cause, but two very plausible solutions. The 1931 disaster is exactly the other way round, with obvious causes but no easy solutions. The European banking crises of 1931 are abundantly easy to explain. There are no academic laurels to be won by finding innovative accounts of causation. The collapses were the result of bank weakness in countries that had been wrecked by the aftermath of bad policies that produced inflation, hyperinflation, and a destruction of banks' balance sheets. An intrinsic vulnerability made for a heightened exposure to political shocks, and disputes about a central European customs union and about the postwar reparations issue were enough to topple a house of cards.

There was something very haphazard about 1931, at least in its origins. Banking crises eventually came to play a major role in the intensification of the depression in the United States, but most U.S. banks were vulnerable because they were small and local. In Europe, however, a decisive stage of the crisis came when megabanks failed, raising almost impossible policy dilemmas for the national governments. The example of the European bank failures of the summer of 1931 in turn translated into a new shock for the U.S. economy, and some of the major money-center banks became vulnerable to investor and depositor panics. Relatively few accounts of the American depression fully take into account the role that the European collapse played in fanning financial uncertainty, in leading banks to call in loans—in short, in pushing the U.S. economy into the Great Depression.[41] In large part this oversight is due to the absence of comparable breakdowns in the second half of the twentieth century. The nonrecurrence of 1931 led many prominent economists to conclude that—as Lawrence Summers and Bradford DeLong put it—"financial and monetary shocks are less important sources of depression than we had suspected."[42]

During the winter of 1930-1931, a number of insiders, notably the Zurich banker Felix Somary, had made the rounds of the financial cognoscenti to deliver grim warnings of the dangers that threatened the German and Italian banking systems.[43] Somewhat ironically, however, the first real sign of major European problems came in Austria rather than in its northern or southern neighbor.

The problems of Austrian banking went back to the aftermath of the First World War and the dissolution of the multinational Habsburg empire, which left a dwarf state contemptuously known as Deutschösterreich. The big banks of the empire needed to adjust to the reduced circumstances of Austrian life. In 1929 the government pressed the largest and most famous of Austrian banks, the Creditanstalt, to merge with an insolvent institution, the Bodenkreditanstalt. All the other Austrian banks had refused a part in this deal, doubtless because of the Bodenkreditanstalt's terrible condition. But the Creditanstalt was bribed into acquiescence. A secret part of the deal was that the Austrian National Bank would make deposits in foreign banks, mostly in the London market, that would be passed on as credits to the Creditanstalt. The amounts thus could be shown as foreign reserves on the balance sheet of the National Bank, while being recycled as support for the largest commercial bank. The governor of the Bank of England, Montagu Norman, called this "tainted money" when, in the aftermath of the collapse, he became aware of the exposure of the British banks in the scheme.[44]

But losses in the commercial bank continued to mount. At any point after 1929, the Creditanstalt might have gone into bankruptcy. In May 1931, the management of the Creditanstalt started to press for an investigation into its assets, arguing that "in view of the continued industrial depression it was necessary to make a conservative valuation of their debtors in order to establish a genuine Balance Sheet." They found losses on their credits of 52 million schillings, and losses on industrial participations of 28 million, in addition to the 60 million in losses they had taken from the Bodenkreditanstalt deal.[45] It is still not quite clear why the directors, at the worst possible moment, were overcome by this sudden urge to be honest and to determine the market valuation of their assets. The most likely explanation is that the leading figure, Zoltan Hajdu, had had some sort of religious conversion experience, and that he felt unable to live with the fundamentally dishonest accounts that his institution had presented for two years.

If the Creditanstalt failure was not immediately necessary, neither was the spread of the crisis to Germany. Although it was a neighbor of Austria, there was little direct German participation in Austrian finance. Indeed German banks held less than 4 percent of the Creditanstalt deposits. But German banks looked like the Austrian banks in that their capital basis had been eroded by inflation and hyperinflation in the early 1920s. And in addition to Germany's incipient banking crisis there was a currency crisis, prompted by the government's attempt to negotiate a customs union with Austria and by its insistence that the postwar reparations settlement be renegotiated.[46]

Then as now, policymakers regarded the financial meltdown as a "crisis of confidence in capitalism" (at the time the phrase was used by the German state secretary Ernest Trendelenburg). "Capitalism" meant presumably the normal functioning of the market. When it breaks down, and needs to be directed politically, a whole range of questions arise, some of them so thorny and controversial that they can easily break apart a fragile political system.

Until the beginning of July 1931, the German authorities and the German central bank had more or less explicitly announced that they would never let a major German bank collapse.[47] Within a few days, however, after it became clear that the British and American central banks were not prepared to assist the German central bank, it took the opposite stance. Thus 1931 unleashed a ferocious debate about regulation, the relationship of financial institutions to the state, and public ownership. The critical discussions took place over one weekend, July 11–12, 1931.

The critical figure in these debates was Jakob Goldschmidt, the head of the Darmstädter und Nationalbank (or Danat Bank) and a master trader, who by 1931 was sitting on the boards of 123 German corporations. He was an extravagantly outgoing figure who in public addresses made himself into the principal exponent of the idea of globalization and openness in 1920s Germany. He explained with a missionary zeal that "the search for private profit is the main driver of economic development, and influences the worker no less than the employer; it will produce through the rise of the individual a higher form of cooperation." A critical part of this process was integrating Germany in the international economy: "We are dependent on the credit of the world, and this credit must find a basis for confidence in the system and in the method. The world must be able to see openly and clearly the developments that influence the behavior of the individual and the community."[48]

There had long been bad feelings among leaders of the major German financial institutions. In particular, the major figures at the rival (and more solid) Deutsche Bank und Disconto Gesellschaft thought that Goldschmidt's business methods and style were profoundly damaging. They too reflected on globalization, and wanted what they thought of as a more German style, a more responsible capitalism than the abrasive Anglo-Saxon style of Goldschmidt. Georg Solmssen, one of the most articulate Deutsche Bank representatives, argued that "the world economy will necessarily, if it wishes to survive, enter a period of mutual respect and agreement about vital fields of interest. This dogma does not deny the right of individual nations to keep their own individuality; it does not mean that the future will belong to a cosmopolitan Esperanto, and that borders determined by geography, history and ethnic difference are destined to disappear."[49]

In June and early July 1931, it became clear that the

Danat had lost a great deal of money, in particular through its exposure to a major textile producer, Nordwolle. Rumors about its insolvency were spreading (and were reported in a Swiss newspaper). Goldschmidt had already found out about the extent of Nordwolle's losses on May 11, by coincidence the day of the Austrian bank failure, as well as that another bank, Dresdner Bank, had extended substantial credits to Nordwolle. As Danat's stock price slipped, it spent its resources buying up its own stock.

On July 10, faced with foreign withdrawals of currency, the German central bank appeared to be running out of usable gold and foreign currency reserves, and announced that it would restrict its support of German banks. The central bank was taking this action in part in response to pressure from the British and U.S. central banks, which were convinced (in large part correctly) that the German problem originated in domestic (German) banks and in companies' moving out of the Reichsmark and into foreign currencies. But with this decision, the position of the Danat became untenable. Oscar Wassermann of Deutsche pointed out to the government that there was a weakness in the Danat, but that the other banks were sound. On Saturday, July 11, 1931, the Danat wrote to the vice president of the German central bank, the Reichsbank, that because of a drain of deposits and the extent of its own share purchases it would be forced to close for business on Monday. The Reichsbank and the Economics Ministry informed the head of the government, Chancellor Heinrich Brüning, who summoned an immediate meeting of ministers and then convened a meeting of bankers in the Chancellery at 9:30 P.M. The bankers defended themselves against accusations that they had given out too much credit, though the principal director of Deutsche Bank added that "private banks, business and the central bank all collectively bore responsibility for this situation."[50] The original proposal of the government—for a government guarantee of the Danat's deposits—looked counterproductive, and most of the participants in the meetings felt that it would simply provoke a run on all the other banks.

Brüning, an austerely pious Catholic politician, later thought that the banks should have restored confidence by extending a network of guarantees on each other's deposits. This idea went back to a suggestion by the Swedish banker Marcus Wallenberg, who had recalled that in 1920 Svenska Handelsbanken had been rescued by a common guarantee of the other large Swedish banks. But in fact, the principal civil servant involved, as well as the head of the

Reichsbank, had said before the bankers were even heard that this proposal (which emanated from the Danat) was unrealizable. When the idea was first brought up, in a discussion in Brüning's office on July 8, the participants had assumed that it would be simply a mechanism to create paper that could be discounted by the central bank.

In 1931, as in 2008, a Swedish solution based on bank cooperation was seen as an answer to crises in much bigger countries such as Germany and the United States. In neither case, however, did the strategy really seem to fit. Sweden was a rather closed society, with a business structure dominated by a very few family firms, who were prepared to trust each other and make deals. Neighborliness and solidarity were much easier there than in the big states, where such virtues were much more prone to erosion. Germany and the United States had big banks that were not run by families, and they competed ruthlessly with each other. They were driven by a mixture of fear—of being sucked into the maelstrom—and the ferocious instinct of driving out a competitor.

On Sunday, July 12, 1931, just before noon, the German ministers met again to hear (from Wassermann of Deutsche Bank) that the second weakest bank, the Dresdner Bank, was on the verge of collapse. Asked whether this was true, the Dresdner Bank managers denied it. In the evening, at 6:30, the bankers came again. The Deutsche Bank suggested that the Danat and Dresdner banks be merged, presumably with a government guarantee that would make clear the dependence of these institutions on the state.

One representative of the government tried to convince Deutsche that it should support the Danat, but Deutsche, worried that it could not determine the extent of the losses, refused. In some contemporary accounts, notably in a detailed journalistic survey, as well as in Goldschmidt's interpretation (which was incorporated into Brüning's memoirs), this appeared as a calculation driven by Deutsche's desire to drive its rival into the dust, even at the price of bringing down the house of cards of German finance.[51] Already on July 6, the chief executive of Deutsche, Oscar Wassermann, had three times talked about the bank issue as the "Danat problem." On the same day, newspaper accounts appeared in Switzerland naming Danat: the leak was widely attributed to Deutsche Bank. And on July 8, Goldschmidt had already visited Wassermann to propose that their banks should merge.

Wassermann in the critical meeting on July 11 simply produced the classical advice that the central bank (Reichsbank) should discount all bills: "The only means of combating a bank run is to pay out." But the Reichsbank refused because it was under pressure from the Bank of England and the Federal Reserve Bank of New York to restrict its credit in order to stem the developing run on the German currency. In that sense, the Reichsbank no longer had operational freedom, but was tied into a network of agreements (above all the gold exchange standard) and operations conducted by other central banks. International cooperation broke down spectacularly in the face of the crisis. The only international financial institution of the time, the Basel-based Bank for International Settlements, had completely inadequate resources.

Brüning was right that a self-organized bank rescue, had it worked, would have saved the government a great deal of trouble. At the same time, the argument of Deutsche that it could not meet an unknown obligation without some sort of public guarantee also seems irrefutable.

The only realistic alternative, but it was a pretty remote straw to grasp, was that France might put up money to help out. The highest official in the Finance Ministry, Hans Schäffer, was pushing for this solution, and had some informal contacts through intermediaries in the financial and journalistic worlds with Pierre Laval, the strongman of the French right. Realistically, however, prospects for success were probably as remote as those for the 2008 idea that China's sovereign wealth fund could bail out American financial institutions.

Some of the initiatives that the German government took had a quite modern ring, and they seem to have been employed swiftly as part of a crisis management strategy. First, the government reorganized the banks, merging the two weakest ones and injecting government money into all of them. Initially, the government tried hard to obtain private money as well, and there were intense negotiations with the leading figures of the powerful Rhine-Ruhr steel lobby, including all of Germany's industrial magnates: Albert Vogler, Friedrich Flick, and Gustav Krupp von Bohlen und Halbach. In the end the business leaders only agreed if the government would put in more money, and if the government advanced them the sums that they were supposed to invest in the recapitalization of Danat Bank. By 1932, 91 percent of the Dresdner Bank's capital, 70 percent of Commerzbank's, and 35 percent of Deutsche's was in public ownership.

Second, the Reichsbank pushed for a new institution that would allow it to discount bills from those banks that could not be traded because the interbank market had stopped operating. This institution, named the Akzept- und Garantiebank, was established with breathtaking speed. It was given a public guarantee in order to provide the additional signature that made bills eligible for Reichsbank lending (rediscounting).

Third, the Reichsbank eventually (in December 1932) created what would now be called a "bad bank" to take over troubled assets whose price no longer corresponded to the value at which they were set in the banks' balance sheet. Two new institutions would take assets off firms' and banks' balance sheets: the first, the Deutsche Finanzierungsinstitut AG, took over up to three-quarters of the bad assets of a bank, but required an annual amortization at 3 percent. The second, the Tilgungskasse für gewerbliche Kredite, required a much lower rate of servicing, only 1 percent, for an initial three-year period, followed by higher rates as economic recovery would set in.

Bailouts are inherently controversial, because they distribute public money in an arbitrary way, to one recipient rather than another. In the United States, Herbert Hoover's innovative Reconstruction Finance

Corporation of 1932 quickly ran into problems because of this issue: it turned out that the credits were going to banks, farms, and businesses that were well connected with Republican politics. Germany offers an even more dramatic example of this kind of problem. As part of the bank bailout in the aftermath of the 1931 crisis, 2.5 million Reichsmarks were put into a small Berlin institution, Hardy & Co., that was a subsidiary of the Dresdner Bank. This money was primarily intended to flow into the electoral campaign coffers of Paul von Hindenburg, the veteran First World War commander who had been elected president of Germany and was standing for reelection in 1932.[52]

In the fragile situation of Weimar politics, it is possible to see how the bailout that was at the center of the government's response to the banking crisis ran into every kind of objection. The claim that the government had been engaged in the "socialization of losses" became an important part of the turbulent electoral campaigns of 1932. In order to get support from the Akzeptbank, banks had to demonstrate that "important economic interests" were at stake, and in practice the majority of Akzeptbank credit went to the savings banks *(Sparkassen)*. It was also used to support enterprises in strategically vital areas, notably Silesia, where the Henckel-Donnersmarck enterprises were treated with special favor. The special issues involved in the support of Silesian industry, and the fear of an opportunistic takeover by foreign issues, led to the Brüning government's most problematic and indeed scandalous rescue operation, the so-called Gelsenberg purchase concluded on the last day that Brüning and his finance minister Hermann Dietrich, the driving force of this bailout, were in office. In this transaction, the government, which as a result of the banking crisis had become Flick's largest creditor, bought out Flick's interest in the steel giant Vereinigte Stahlwerke. Dietrich's former state secretary Hans Schäffer referred to the operation as "extreme stupidity."[53]

We can see the same crippling effects of a bailout in the comparatively much more expensive and extensive case of Austria, where the collapse of the Creditanstalt in May 1931 precipitated the more general central European financial collapse. The government's answer involved taking over the bank, and eventually merging it with other weakened Austrian banks, the Wiener Bankverein and the Niederösterreichische Escompte Gesellschaft. The subsidy was expensive, amounting to 9 to 10 percent of GNP (substantially less than the cost of bailouts for Mexico or Japan in the 1990s, but comparable to the projected costs of the 2008 U.S. bailout). Since the Credit-anstalt held major stakes in some 142 Austrian firms, it meant that the government through the bank was in effect running most of Austrian business. Like modern bailouts in emerging markets, it was also accompanied by massive corruption, the revelation of which became the stock-in-trade of the opposition Nazi movement in Austria. Then, as now, there was massive public hostility to the idea of a bailout, in that it appeared to be a form of support for the institutions and people responsible for the crisis.[54]

The cost of bailouts, even when they seemed to have been administered promptly and with high efficiency as in the German case, thus seemed extreme. Implementing the bailouts also brought the state into a series of contentious micro-level decisions on the health of particular enterprises and on the fate of individual bank directors. Given the poisonous ideological backdrop of anti-Semitism in the context of central Europe in the 1930s, it is unsurprising that this radical doctrine was fanned by the character of the government's response to banking crises, and that both in Germany and more explicitly in Austria a process of expropriating Jewish property ("aryanization") that was at first called Germanization or Austrianization set in even before the Nazis took power in those countries. The episodes of managing bank failures in retrospect look like the beginning of a process of state domination, corruption, and even racial persecution that would become ever more menacing.

The central European crises were the beginning, not the end of financial contagion. The threat to U.K. investment banks ("merchant banks") because of their exposure to central Europe was one crucial factor in the speculative attack that built up after July on the British pound, and forced Britain to abandon the gold standard commitment on September 21, 1931.[55] From this relatively late stage in the Great Depression, the drama of currency realignments took center stage. It soon became clear that devaluations produced in many countries an improved trade performance, as import prices rose and export prices fell, and many commentators saw in currency manipulation essentially a zero-sum trade war strategy. But departures from the gold standard in countries that were not large debtors also produced enhanced financial stability, and eliminated some of the disruptive flows of "hot money." The British departure from gold, for example, ended its incipient banking crisis.

Speculative attacks now began to hit the dollar, prompting withdrawals from larger New York banks. In this way, international elements played a key role in the second half of the American depression. After President Roosevelt also abandoned the gold standard, speculative attacks shifted. The banks and the currencies of the remaining gold standard countries (the so-called Gold Bloc)—Belgium, France, the Netherlands, and Switzerland—were now vulnerable. Only the end of the fixed-exchange-rate regime removed the vulnerability.

Every kind of international coordination of policy against the economic collapse failed. Some of the proposed schemes were intellectually appealing and innovative. One of the boldest took the form of a private-public partnership to overcome the problem of limited resources in the official sector. In the spring of 1931, as the crisis was threatening to explode, a Belgian banker proposed working in a public-private package with the Swedish financier Ivar Kreuger. Kreuger had built up an enormous business on the back of his Svenska Tändsticks match company, a monopoly that had allowed him to leverage loans to countries in a precarious state. But Kreuger's empire was increasingly fragile, and skeptics began to suspect that the collateral that he had pledged in order to raise money was forged. Less than a year after the Bank for International Settlements had contemplated this bold stroke of public-private financing, on March 12, 1932, Kreuger killed himself in his Paris apartment.

Oscar Rydbeck, director of the major Swedish bank Skandinaviska Banken and a close associate of Kreuger's, wrote soon after his death that "Towards the end he seems to have lost all idea of the value of figures. . . . It has been suggested to people like myself that we ought to have gone properly into all the figures and not have taken them for granted, but a member of a board of directors does not go behind his chief and ask the clerks in the firm if the figures Kreuger has given are correct."[56] Shortly before Kreuger killed himself, the Swedish government attempted to draw up a rescue package for the Kreuger business, and approached the rival business group of the Wallenberg family, around the Skandinaviska Enskilda Banken, for assistance in putting it together. But Marcus Wallenberg recorded his reply as follows: "The Prime Minister said that his confidence in SEB's management was greater than that of the other banks and that this was the real reason why he was anxious to have SEB participate in this transaction. . . . for similar reasons, [I] wanted to stay away from the deal."[57] The lesson was clear: private-public partnerships were practically impossible, because no one knew whom to trust.

OUTLOOK

Very quickly, 1931 was seen as a watershed. Among the eloquent statements about the new world created by state intervention in currency determination and financial intermediation is a reflection by the great Hamburg banker Carl Melchior, while walking in St. James's Park in London. He was taking a break from a conference summoned to negotiate a moratorium on German external debt, where it was decided that German borrowers should be temporarily protected from their creditors because of Germany's national foreign-exchange shortage and not because of individual insolvency or illiquidity. Melchior complained: "What we have just experienced is a destruction of the rules of the game of the capitalist system, which depend on strict observance. This is the first time that I have had to refuse the compliance with a signature that I gave voluntarily, because the state requires this of me. Believe me, I know Germany. The capitalist system in Germany cannot cope with this breach of the rules of the game. Things will go further and further until we are in the abyss." At the time (but not later), Melchior's interlocutor, a German finance ministry official, found this verdict "exaggerated."[58]

There was an easy answer to the 1929 collapse that could be and was applied in the case of subsequent crises, notably the stock market crash of 1987 and the dot-com crash of 2000–2001. Because the same man, Alan Greenspan, was as chairman of the Federal Reserve Board responsible for U.S. monetary policy in both these episodes, this well-established response even became known as the "Greenspan put." Monetary loosening was an easy answer, and it was learned well.

The responses to "1931" were much more complicated and messy. The crisis of 1931 was also a powerful scare story, and it haunted many policymakers as well as economists in the years after the Second World War. Because it had driven the reversal of globalization so completely, everyone concluded (rightly) that it was vital to avoid such a crisis, since it could not really be managed at all.

The drama had a geopolitical component, in that it was really only conceivable that a very large and dominant state could act in such a way as to take responsibility for the system as a whole.[59] Since the international lender of last resort has to set aside its own short-term interests, or those of its citizens, in order to take a longer-term stake in the well-being of the international community, this role is hard for a democracy, except in very peculiar circumstances. It may have been easier for an oligarchically dominated Great Britain to take this responsibility in the eighteenth and nineteenth centuries than it was for the democratic United States in the 1920s and 1930s.

There were two alternative philosophies about avoiding a repetition of "1931." One argued that the character of the crisis lay in the dramatic reversal of credit flows. In the 1920s, capital had moved massively from the United States (and to some extent from the United Kingdom) to central Europe and South America; in the 1930s, there was a flow back, from the crisis-struck recipients of the previous decade back to the United States. The unstable flows indicated that capital movements were in themselves destabilizing. Containing and limiting capital flows could thus limit the scope for the international transmission of crises. A check on capital movements had also opened the way for the management of monetary and fiscal policy in a distinctly national context. These ideas about limiting capital mobility were at the heart of the settlement reached at the

1944 United Nations monetary conference at Bretton Woods, and remained the guiding principles of international economic management during the first two and a half postwar decades.

The second interpretation of how to avoid "1931" is fundamentally more recent, though it was anticipated by some 1930s writers, notably the Austrian economist Gottfried Haberler.[60] In this view, the fixed-exchange-rate system, as revived by central bankers in the 1920s, was at the heart of the problem. It created mismatches in which banks and other corporations built up debt in one internationally traded currency (dollars or British pounds), but had assets in their own domestic currency, Austrian schillings or German Reichsmarks. To some extent, the difficulties could be avoided by ending the fixed-exchange-rate system and adopting flexible rates. (Historically, too, there existed a clear link between the fixed-exchange-rate regime and vulnerability to currency crises.) But such a solution produced new problems, which became especially clear in the discussion of emerging market crises of the 1990s. The predicament of the borrowing countries was now termed "original sin" (by Barry Eichengreen and Ricardo Hausmann), in that residents of countries with poorly developed financial systems could not borrow long-term in their own currencies, and were thus necessarily exposed to foreign exchange risk (and with it, the potential for 1931-style blowups).[61] The solution, then, lay in developing adequate or sophisticated financial systems.

Early in the twenty-first century, good and deep financial institutions were developed to prevent the recurrence of a "1931," along with a monetary policy that was supposed to avoid a "1929." But even with good financial institutions, there were powerful incentives for borrowers to borrow as cheaply as possible, and this meant frequently borrowing in a foreign currency and incurring an exchange rate risk. In 2008, it became fully apparent that none of the existing mechanisms that might prevent a "1931" were as effective as their adherents thought them to be.

3

THE CRASH OF 2008: THE
WEEKENDS THAT MADE HISTORY

THE DRAMATIC WEEKENDS in March 2008 and September 2008 are the modern equivalents of 1929 and 1931 in the earlier debate about the causes of interwar deglobalization. And yes, there is a clear connection between them—one that is much more direct than the tenuous link between 1929 and 1931. In March 2008, stock prices fell sharply, and one major institution was at risk of failure, but was rescued by the government and a larger financial institution. The central bank responded by pumping liquidity into the market, and expectations were stabilized. But the failure of a big investment bank in September brought the whole system down. At the beginning of the year, there was a clear belief that the 2008 crisis could be tackled in the same way that 1929 should have been managed, and as 1987 and 2001 had in fact been resolved. But reproducing the older answers did not work. By the end of 2008, there remained exactly that feeling of hopelessness and of the inadequacy of domestic and international governmental mechanisms that the crisis of 1931 had produced.

The story of 2008 and 2009, as well as of the Great Depression, is highly unusual. Most of the crises of the nineteenth-century gold standard world, as well as of the integrated economy of the later twentieth century, arose in peripheral countries, and the principal task that policymakers in the major industrial countries assigned themselves was preventing the crisis from doing damage at the financial center. By contrast, the Great Depression and the post-2007 crisis attacked the central structures of the most financially advanced economies.

The credit crisis, which made an initial appearance in early 2007, originally involved the subprime mortgage sector—in other words, a rather limited part of the U.S. housing market (although in the previous decade, its share in the U.S. market had risen from under a twentieth to about a fifth). Mortgages had been issued for low-income borrowers, with minimal or no down-payment requirements, very lax certifications of income levels, and low initial repayment schedules. These mortgages were then securitized and repackaged, with a differentiation into tranches to reflect different default probabilities. At the end of

February 2007, the U.S. government–sponsored Federal Home Loan Mortgage Corporation (Freddie Mac) announced that it would stop buying the most risky subprime mortgages; and at the beginning of April a leading subprime mortgage lender, New Century Financial Corporation, filed for Chapter 11 bankruptcy. At the end of July, the large New York investment bank Bear Stearns liquidated two hedge funds that had invested in mortgage-backed securities. Even so, it was hard to see how losses from a sector that amounted to around $625 billion could threaten the entire financial system of the United States or of the world. The estimates of losses on subprime mortgages were very low even late in the development of the crisis: $45 billion in April 2008 and $50 billion in October.[1]

The first signs that there might be major problems for banks came in Europe, not in the United States, with the failure of two relatively small German institutions. The first to go under was the IKB Deutsche Industriebank, which was partly owned by a state development bank that had originally been created after the Second World War to finance German recovery, and had a substantial exposure to U.S. debt via an Irish-based subsidiary. It required an initial €8 billion rescue. Almost immediately came the larger case of another publicly owned bank, the Landesbank Girozentrale Sachsen, which needed a €17.3 billion emergency line of credit.

These apparently isolated incidents led nevertheless to generalized worry about the stability of banking institutions, and many banks started to fear the illiquidity or insolvency of a counterparty. The European Central Bank, as well as the Federal Reserve System, started to provide very large amounts of liquidity to the market, while the Bank of England believed there was less need for such action; the major British banks simply accessed the European Central Bank's liquidity via their subsidiaries in the Eurozone. Smaller institutions, however, were not able to do this. In September, one of them, Northern Rock, facing a classic bank run, appealed for emergency support from the Bank of England, and was eventually (in February 2008) taken into public ownership.

Over the course of 2008 a surprise development emerged: liquidity provision on its own was insufficient to stem the crisis of confidence, and a more systemic solution to the problem of banking instability was needed. The turning points of the drama were two tension-filled weekends in New York: the first occurred in the spring, when the Federal Reserve stepped in to rescue the threatened investment bank

Bear Stearns on March 14. It provided $29 billion in financing at its primary credit rate for JPMorgan Chase to buy Bear Stearns. The action was interpreted as a sign that Wall Street had failed, but also as an indication of the willingness of the government and the regulatory authorities to step in with dramatic measures that stretched the legal limits on their capacity for action. Debates about what could or should be done highlighted not only the powerlessness of governments (as well as of financial institutions) in the face of the market slide, but also the great demand for government action and the assertion of government power.

As in 1929, when the markets were gripped by the historical memory of 1907, and the hope that J. P. Morgan would organize a rescue of the market, there looked as if there was a specific historic parallel that held out some hope. In October 1998, after the emerging-market crisis had spilled out from East Asia to affect Russia and Brazil, the Connecticut-based firm Long-Term Capital Management (LTCM) had been on the verge of collapse. In a weekend of crisis negotiations, the Federal Reserve Bank of New York managed to induce eleven major financial institutions, which were threatened by huge losses stemming from LTCM's insolvency, to mount a rescue operation of $3.625 billion. The Fed itself put in no money. The creditor banks throughout the negotiations were highly suspicious of the motivations and actions of their competitors. One, Bear Stearns, refused to join in the rescue scheme. Another, Goldman Sachs, which the others suspected of planning a separate action with Warren Buffett, later underwent a palace coup in which Henry Paulson replaced Jon Corzine as CEO. Self-help was already quite problematic in 1998.[2]

Nevertheless, some large institutions also took self-help measures in the early phases of the 2007–2008 crisis. On October 15, 2007, the large retail banks Citigroup, Bank of America, and JPMorgan Chase established a "master liquidity enhancement conduit" to buy assets from their existing off-balance-sheet vehicles. But such steps were inadequate as the prices of securities fell, and questions about solvency began to arise. The idea of self-help disintegrated.

On February 14, 2008, the general situation with regard to mortgage-backed securities deteriorated as the giant Swiss bank UBS announced a fourth quarter loss of $11.3 billion. The loss stemmed from the writing off of $13.7 billion in U.S. mortgages, and revealed the extent of its exposure to the Alt-A mortgage market. Margin calls began to bring down smaller institutions with big mortgage holdings, and at the beginning of March, rumors began to circulate that a big European bank would not be a counterparty to overnight financing for Bear Stearns. During the week of March 10, a slow-motion collapse began.[3] There was a big increase in puts on Bear Stearns shares, presumably because counterparties were trying to insure themselves against losses in the event it failed. The U.S. Office of the Comptroller of the Currency began asking even small banks about the extent of their exposure to Bear Stearns. On Tuesday, March 11, the Federal Reserve announced that it would begin to make up to $200 billion in Treasury securities available through the Term Securities Lending Facility on March 27, but it soon became clear that this date was too far in the future to help Bear Stearns. Goldman Sachs initially refused, and then agreed, to take over positions in Bear Stearns held by a Dallas hedge fund, and both moves heightened the prevailing doubt about the viability of the smallest and weakest of the five big New York investment banks.

By Wednesday evening, the situation looked hopeless, and during the night of March 13 to 14, the Federal Reserve put together what was initially thought to be a rescue package, in which it would make funds available through its discount window, not directly to Bear, but to J. P. Morgan, which as a universal bank regulated by the Federal Reserve System had access to central bank lending. The Fed hoped this would give enough time for an orderly sale, but over the weekend it became clear that the funding demands caused by the calling of loans were too great for the bank to reopen on Monday, and a sale to J. P. Morgan was negotiated at the humiliating price of $2 a share. J. P. Morgan's analysts concluded that more than $220 billion of the $300 billion in assets might be toxic. The Federal Reserve provided $30 billion of secured lending, which would be used to buy the most toxic assets. The Fed also granted exemptions from its rules to allow J. P. Morgan to extend credit and guarantees to Bear Stearns and to exempt these from its capital leverage ratio.

There was no time for alternative purchasers to make offers for all or parts of the Bear Stearns business. Subsequently, after pressure from Bear Stearns employees and shareholders, and amid uncertainty about the commitment of J. P. Morgan for the Bear balance sheet, the share price was revised to $12 a share. Unlike the solution worked out for Long-Term

Capital Management, the $30 billion credit line from the Federal Reserve meant that this was in effect a government bailout.

The crisis weekends of 2008 were widely recognized as dramatic inflections of the world economic order, just as surely as some contemporaries recognized the significance of 1931. Martin Wolf wrote on March 26, 2008, in his *Financial Times* column:

> Remember Friday March 14, 2008: it was the day the dream of global free-market capitalism died. For three decades we have moved towards market-driven financial systems. By its decision to rescue Bear Stearns, the Federal Reserve, the institution responsible for monetary policy in the U.S., chief protagonist of free-market capitalism, declared this era over. It showed in deeds its agreement with the remark by Josef Ackermann, chief executive of Deutsche Bank, that "I no longer believe in the market's self-healing power." Deregulation has reached its limits.[4]

Former Federal Reserve chairman Paul Volcker told the Economic Club of New York on April 8, 2008: "Simply stated, the bright new financial system—for all its talented participants, for all its rich rewards—has failed the test of the market place. To meet the challenge, the Federal Reserve judged it necessary to take actions that extend to the very edge of its lawful and implied powers, transcending certain long embedded central banking principles and practices."[5] Later in the year, his successor Alan Greenspan explained to Congress that "I found a flaw in the model that I perceived is the critical functioning structure that defines how the world works. That's precisely the reason I was shocked . . . I still do not fully understand why it happened, and obviously to the extent that I figure it happened and why, I will change my views."[6]

The saving of Bear Stearns and the increased lending activity of the Federal Reserve did not stop the spread of problems in the financial sector. By July 2008, Fannie Mae and Freddie Mac were obviously in trouble. There was enormous foreign pressure for the U.S. government to intervene, especially from the big emerging markets that had become big holders of U.S. securities. The Chinese government was extremely anxious, and Russian leader Vladimir Putin even made a personal telephone call to President Bush to ask for support of these housing institutions. On July 13 (incidentally the day of the German collapse of 1931), the Federal Reserve Board authorized lending to Fannie Mae and Freddie Mac and the Treasury obtained a temporary authorization to buy equity in these institutions. Under the terms of the Housing and Recovery Act (signed on July 30), the Treasury was authorized to buy obligations of Fannie Mae and Freddie Mac, and these government-sponsored enterprises (GSEs) were placed under the regulatory authority of a new Federal Housing Finance Agency. On September 7, they were placed under government "conservatorship"—in effect, nationalized.

Investment banks also had problems, with the next weakest bank after Bear Stearns looking like the next domino in a precarious row. Since March 14, the share price of Lehman Brothers had continually weakened. The fall accelerated after it announced a $2.8 billion loss. Its chairman and CEO, Richard Fuld, who was popularly called "the gorilla," became increasingly withdrawn. There had been some desultory talks about increased cooperation with some other financial giant, such as the insurance group AIG, years before the crisis. At the end of 2007, he had reportedly said that "as long as I am alive this firm will never be sold. And if it is sold after I die, I will reach back from the grave and prevent it."[7] But in private in June and July 2008, Fuld began talking about a management buyout. He also discussed selling Lehman's vast and increasingly problematic property portfolio.

The losses continued to mount. At the beginning of August he held discussions with leading executives from the Korea Development Bank and from China's Citic Securities. But the foreign investors found Lehman's negotiators unhelpful, and Fuld was unwilling to give any details about Lehman's operations. Not surprisingly, they walked away from any deal. Finally, in the second week of September, Lehman started a different strategy and started to explore selling off the property portfolio as a "bad bank." In the course of the week, with expectations of a third-quarter loss of $4 billion, the share price fell by another half.

When Treasury Secretary Henry Paulson and the Federal Reserve Bank of New York President Timothy Geithner, at an hour's notice, called a meeting of leading financial figures in New York on the evening of September 12, most assumed that the major theme would be the rescue of Lehman. The main headline of the *Financial Times* that morning had been "Lehman Race to Find a Buyer." The most obvious candidates to buy Lehman were Bank of America and the British bank Barclays. They started intense preparations for a deal on that Friday in separate New York law offices—Sullivan and Cromwell, and Simpson Thacher. The Friday meeting was intended to launch a more profound series of rescue negotiations that would be conducted the next morning. In the same way as market participants in October 1929 were mesmerized by the memory of 1907, and J. P. Morgan's brilliantly successful coordination of a bank rescue, the precedent that obsessed the financial markets in 2008 was the October 1998 rescue of Long-Term Capital Management. That had been orchestrated by the Federal Reserve Bank, and had as its major feature bankers putting money into a common rescue fund.

Saturday, September 13, 2008, turned out very differently. Instead of a 1907 or a 1998, in which a group of bankers recognized the extent of their common interests, it evolved into a game of speed-dating. The leading figures were looking for bilateral deals that would protect them from the financial storm. Any institution that did not manage a permanent hookup was doomed.

By Saturday, it looked to the Lehman bankers as if Bank of America was no longer listening to them. Fuld's efforts to reach the Bank of America CEO in Charlottesville were unsuccessful, and his calls were simply left unreturned, because Kenneth Lewis was now engaged with a different partner. Fuld complained: "I can't believe that son of a bitch won't return my calls." The CEO of Merrill Lynch, John

Thain, in what at the time was lauded as a brilliant move, had contacted CEO Lewis, suggesting a sale of a 9.9 percent stake in Merrill. He had concluded that among the big investment banks, Merrill was the next in line to fall, after Bear Stearns and Lehman. Thain is reported to have exclaimed: "This could be me sitting here next Friday."[8] The Bank of America team that had been looking at Lehman was told to fly back to New York to look at Merrill instead. But it insisted that it was not interested in buying a minority stake, but would only contemplate a purchase of the entire business.

Merrill executives also talked to Goldman Sachs managers about Goldman taking a relatively small stake in its rival, as well as with Morgan Stanley, which together with Goldman was one of only two large investment banks remaining. The discussions continued in law offices and apartments until the early hours of Sunday, and the meeting at the New York Fed resumed again at 9 A.M. These alternative "dates" with Goldman or Morgan Stanley in the end were not needed, because by Sunday afternoon Bank of America had agreed to buy Merrill for $50 billion. Merrill's board accepted the offer via a telephone meeting at 6 P.M. The chairman of the Federal Reserve Board, Ben Bernanke, and Treasury Secretary Paulson subsequently placed great pressure on Bank of America not to back out of the deal.

Already on Saturday, the last hope of Lehman collapsed when it became clear that the British government would not provide a bridging guarantee to Barclays if the U.S. government was not prepared to something similar. As a consequence all the possible deals broke down and less than forty-eight hours remained to prepare a hugely complex bankruptcy filing. Some estimates suggested later that as much as $75 billion of the value of Lehman was destroyed simply by the rapidity of the bankruptcy deal, which created a cascade of defaults at subsidiaries as 900,000 separate derivatives contracts were cancelled. Since much of the trading was automated, some contracts escaped attention.[9] A German publicly owned bank, for instance, was still transferring money to Lehman on Monday, after the declaration of bankruptcy.

Paulson wanted initially to portray the failure of Lehman as a demonstration of his commitment to the principles of a market economy, his opposition to a bailout culture, and his willingness to show the essential health of the American financial system by its capacity to withstand a brutal test. The day after the bankruptcy, he declared, "I never considered it appropriate to put taxpayer money on the line in resolving Lehman Brothers."[10] Before the crisis, laissez-faire commentators had urged Paulson to "take this weekend off" and show that the previous rescues of Fannie Mae and Freddie Mac were unique.[11] On Monday morning, some continued to applaud the U.S. government's noninterference. But very soon the ramifications of this policy stance became apparent. By the end of the day Monday, Paulson was trying to relativize his strict opposition to bailouts, and when asked about the possibility of federal rescues, said "Don't read it as 'no more.'"[12]

As an initial measure, new central bank facilities were needed to support the market. On September 14, the Federal Reserve Board extended the range of collateral it was prepared to accept for the Primary Dealer Credit Facility (already established in March, and at that time limited to investment-grade debt securities). The rapidity of the Lehman collapse and the scale of its losses were clearly problems not just for Lehman, but also for every financial institution that had dealings with it. Lehman had about $130 billion in outstanding bonds. As a consequence of its exposure to Lehman, one of the oldest and safest money market funds, the Reserve Primary Fund, saw its shares fall below the one-dollar level—and by "breaking the buck" threaten the security of what had been assumed to be a foolproof investment. The remaining investment banks became highly vulnerable. Morgan Stanley experienced withdrawals by hedge funds of more than $100 billion. Within days, both Morgan Stanley and Goldman had ceased to be investment banks and filed to reorganize as bank holding groups regulated by the Federal Reserve.

Above all, the failure of Lehman immediately hit American International Group (AIG), an insurance company regulated as an insurance company by New York State, but behaving in practice like a bank that could take big risks on the basis of a very large balance sheet. The problem was that AIG had written over $400 billion in derivative contracts, mostly credit default swaps that protected other institutions' holdings of a wide range of securities. These swaps were supposed to guarantee only the most secure, so-called super-senior notes, which would not have problems unless all the other investors were completely destroyed. AIG had calculated that they would only face losses if 40 percent of U.S. homeowners defaulted on their mortgages. The securities were consequently widely regarded as invulnerable, and the writing of these contracts provided a steady stream of fee income, with an annual premium of over $200 million (or 0.05 percent of the amount insured, indicating how relatively risk-free this business was supposed to be). Indeed the head of AIG Financial Products, which marketed the protection, explained in August 2007 that the company could not envisage any scenario that would "see us losing $1 in any of those transactions."[13] Now a failure of AIG risked bringing down every institution that had insured its credit risk. So by Tuesday, the U.S. government effectively took over AIG in an $85 billion bailout. At least $12.9 billion went to Goldman Sachs, and very large amounts to other major financial institutions. The real price tag of the AIG rescue kept on rising as its credit default contracts fell due. By March 2009, government support of AIG amounted to over $165 billion, and the government decided to break up the company.

The broader aspects of a bank rescue plan remained shrouded in uncertainty, with frequent policy reversals. The initial approach of the U.S. Treasury was to push for the creation of a fund with which it would buy distressed assets, so that they could be taken off the balance sheets of banks, and banks could resume their normal lending. The initial version of the Troubled Asset Relief Plan (TARP) was first rejected, and then passed on October 3 in a modified form by the U.S. Congress, after operatic histrionics in which Paulson fell down on his knees before Speaker of the House Nancy Pelosi. The TARP was supposed to involve $700 billion, but in practice its effectiveness was quickly destroyed by disputes about the appropriate valuation of assets, and the money was not used. The problem with values stemmed from the need to in effect replace or second-guess the market. If the values were priced at the current market values, which had been driven down by panic, the banks would receive no significant relief, and they would contract their lending still further. But if the prices paid reflected some expectation of what might eventually be realized (with assumptions of a rapid return to a more benign economic environment), the result would be a major subsidy. In addition, the assets concerned were not homogenous in the sense that a Treasury bill is a general liability of the U.S. government, but were the product of repackaging diverse and quite specific liabilities. Consequently, every asset was fundamentally different, and needed to be valued individually—which would obviously be a very difficult task. Doubts about the feasibility of the original TARP thus caused it to be pushed aside on October 14 in favor of a government recapitalization of major financial institutions. As much as $250 billion was supposed to be provided in this way, and nine large banks immediately were pressed by the U.S. Treasury to sign up for $125 billion in recapitalization.

The morphing of the TARP into a recapitalization plan did not restart bank lending. So over the next months, aspects of the original plan were revived, and more radical alternatives, such as a complete nationalization of the banks, were discussed. The purchase of troubled assets, however, still was a major part of the plan announced on February 10, 2009, by Timothy Geithner, Treasury secretary of the new Obama administration.

Despite the bailout, a surge of money into safe Treasury securities continued. In addition, the American crisis produced some unexpected casualties. Like the interwar story, a catastrophe in one country triggered other collapses. Emerging markets were hit by the disappearance of funds from investors who had earlier been searching for risk and higher returns. As those countries began to contemplate the dramatic reversal of international capital streams, economic prospects elsewhere suddenly darkened as well. These problems of emerging markets in turn hit the big exporters, especially Japan and Germany, that specialized in engineering and machine tool solutions, and that had been the major beneficiaries of the spreading industrialization that followed from economic globalization.

The models that were discussed for solving the U.S. crisis were taken from other countries. Both Britain and France launched a compulsory state recapitalization of major financial institutions; the United States then also imposed a compulsory Capital Purchase Program within the TARP, in which the government acquired warrants and preferred shares, injecting $145 billion into nine large banks. Another alternative involved merging weak banks into stronger ones, usually with some added measure of government support. The British retail bank Halifax Bank of Scotland (HBOS) protected itself by merging with another British bank, Lloyds TSB, in a takeover valued at £12.2 billion, with the British government supporting Lloyds. Finally, although the original vision of the TARP failed to materialize, the idea that banking health could only be fully restored once the balance sheets were cleaned remained persuasive. In particular, there were attractive precedents in the Swedish and Norwegian solutions of the early 1990s, which involved establishing a "bad bank" to take over and manage problematic bank debt.

Though the large foreign players that had been active investors in U.S. financial institutions earlier in the year now stood aside, there remained some very large private actors who still believed that they might play some stabilizing role. On September 24, 2008, Warren Buffett put $5 billion into Goldman Sachs. But he also warned that a failure to implement the U.S. government's scheme would be an "economic Pearl Harbor." Buffett's plan was not a private rescue, but a bet on a new kind of public-private partnership that might be used to respond to the crisis.

The crisis very quickly became a global one, and discussions about a resolution took on an apocalyptic tone. On October 11, the head of the IMF told the G-7 finance ministers meeting in Washington, "Intensifying solvency concerns about a number of the largest U.S.-based and European financial institutions have pushed the global financial system to the brink of systemic meltdown."[14]

THE CHALLENGE TO GLOBALIZATION

The sharpening of the financial crisis quickly led to deglobalization effects that recall some of the most discouraging moments of the twentieth-century Great Depression: a reduction in flows of capital and trade, and in movements of people.

First, the 2008 crisis produced profound doubts about the desirability of international financial connectedness. In particular, if banks are to depend on government authorities for "lender of last resort" operations, or for selling bad assets from their balance sheets, or for recapitalization (the three different channels with which national governments have in various ways dealt with the banking crisis), there will be pressure from governments on banks to expand lending, but primarily in a national context. The fact that very large foreign counterparties—Deutsche Bank, Crédit Lyonnais, and UBS—were the beneficiaries of the AIG rescue became part of a major political scandal.

In the early 1930s, one of the major themes of critics of Wall Street was that they had corruptly sent American money to dangerous and unstable areas, notably South America and Central Europe, and in the process had received handsome fees from the issue of bonds, but bore little long-term risk. In 2009, British prime minister Gordon Brown complained about the international activities of failed banks such as the Royal Bank of Scotland: "Almost all their losses are in subprime mortgages in America and related to the acquisition of [the Dutch bank] ABN Amro. These are irresponsible risks taken by the bank with people's money in the UK." He added that the decision to buy ABN "was wrong."[15] An important part of the rescue operation of the Royal Bank of Scotland was the selling off of foreign branches and activities. Elsewhere there was a similar pattern. Italian and Austrian banks had few domestic problems, but had experienced massive losses as a consequence of earlier large-scale purchases of banks in central Europe. The American giant Citigroup, which had established a presence in more than a hundred countries, would also be slimmed down and its foreign exposure reduced, even though the large losses stemmed primarily from its U.S. business. Internationalism made for political vulnerability, so finance was pushed to become more national.

In Europe, the financial crisis has thrown up a particular problem that was long familiar, but assumed to be largely academic. During the 1980s, a single internal market was created, and capital restrictions were lifted. In the 1990s, Europe moved to adopt a single currency. This decades-long political push to integration established a largely integrated money and capital market, with banks extending their activities across national frontiers.

In particular, the reconstruction of central Europe after the collapse of communism often involved the entry of foreign banks with more efficient and modernized business models. An Italian bank, UniCredit, for example, bought Bank Austria, which had been among the most dynamic European banks in the central European market in the 1990s and had bought up a large portfolio of post-communist financial institutions. But the regulation and supervision of the banks remained national prerogatives, and many countries continued to insist on their national idiosyncrasies as an argument against a common supervisor and regulator. As long as there was no urgent crisis, there seemed to be no need to address this problem.

Resistance to Europe-wide regulation also had a clear political logic. Potential bank rescues would require fiscal action to absorb losses and recapitalize the banks, and this could not be the domain of the European Central Bank, which would not have enough resources, but must be that of national governments and national taxpayers. In consequence, even the high-level taskforce under the eminent former governor of the Banque de France, Jacques de Larosière, which had been assembled to propose a European regulatory solution, drew back because it feared that such a plan would be "unrealistic." Instead it proposed merely a European Systemic Reason composed of central bankers who, under the auspices of the European Central Bank, would analyze and warn against potential risks.

When the crisis broke out in 2008, it was too late for preventive regulatory measures. Disentangling complicated cross-national banking arrangements proved to be complicated and acutely painful. The complex attempts to take apart a Belgian-Dutch bank, Fortis, led to the collapse of the Belgian government. Central and East European countries, which during the boom years of the early twenty-first century had borrowed heavily in foreign currencies, and from foreign institutions, were now very vulnerable. The borrowers, who found servicing and repayment harder as currencies plummeted against the euro and the Swiss franc, called for a nationalization of finance, and in effect for an expropriation of the creditors. The financial rescue discussions took place against a deteriorating macroeconomic background, which threatened the fiscal positions of those governments attempting to recast banking systems.

The financial crisis had a second deglobalization effect: it slowed, and in some cases halted, commerce. The drying up of bank credit, especially in the wake of the collapse of Lehman, made trade financing very difficult. Many rich industrial countries have semiofficial financing institutions that can give export guarantees, but few emerging markets have this kind of protection. As a consequence, many Asian or Latin American producers could not sell their goods to the advanced world, even though there may have been customers who wanted to buy them. In turn, they no longer were able to buy the machine tools or other engineering products that they might have needed to continue to expand their productive capacity. The endangering even of one side of a trade relationship means that some deals will not be concluded. The exports of those countries that specialized most in highly specialized tools—Japan and Germany—were the most dramatically affected by the collapse of exports in the last quarter of 2008. The financial crisis resembled a heart attack that suddenly cut off the circulating medium of the world.

As a consequence, during the fourth quarter of 2008, in the wake of the Lehman collapse, there occurred the sharpest decline in industrial output since the Second World War, a pace of decline sharper even than that experienced during the collapses of the Great Depression. In particular, the world's large export economies, Germany, Japan, Korea, were badly hit.

It might be possible to argue that even such a powerful shock is only temporary, that the rapid downward spiral of trade is caused by a destocking process as inventories are reduced, and that a solid demand for trade finance might indeed be one of the ways that the credit engine is restarted. But this optimistic view ignores one of the crucial elements of the deglobalization spiral: as trade falls, people want to reduce their dependence on trade. Another way of putting this point, which was frequently raised as an argument during the Great Depression, is that protective trade measures can be a weapon in a struggle against the consequences of monetary chaos. Even in the 1930s, few argued unashamedly for protection, and almost everyone recognized that trade protection was not an ideal approach to economic policymaking. But it might represent a very satisfactory second-best solution because it can stop the propagation of deflation across national frontiers.[16]

Today rising levels of unemployment are leading straightforwardly to a demand for trade protection, a sentiment buttressed by an argument similar to that advanced for "financial patriotism." That is, if governments are to step in as the rescuers of the economy, and apply large-scale Keynesian solutions of the type advocated in the 1930s, they will want to ensure that the benefits of the stimulus packages are concentrated in the national economy. An open economy produces a "leaky Keynesianism," in which demand trickles out of the national container, and seems to create jobs in other countries and for people paying other taxes. It is not surprising that in the 1930s, the assertion of Keynesianism went hand-in-hand with demands for national self-sufficiency.[17]

In the modern world, there is a deep rhetorical aversion to the language of national self-sufficiency, at least among the political elite, but there is also a practical desire to protect local jobs and local business. Even in 2009, opinion surveys in industrial countries indicate widespread basic support for the principles of free trade; but protectionist arguments come in a new way, as accompaniments to the discussion of countercyclical fiscal strategy. The controversy over the "Buy America" clauses of the February 2009 stimulus package pitted the legislature against the executive in a way absolutely familiar to students of the 1930s (and immortalized in a classic book by Elmer Schattschneider).[18] Eventually many of the central elements of this demand were scaled back. This was the dilemma that Roosevelt's Reciprocal Trade Agreements Act, which combined industrial reorganization efforts with trade-liberalization measures, was designed to solve.

As with financial nationalism, again the most intractable problems with protectionism are occurring in Europe. France in 2008 initially made the rescue of its automobile industry dependent on producers' moving production from Slovakia back to France. It was prohibited from enforcing these provisions after an intervention by the European Union, but French producers repatriated production anyway in accordance with the preferences of the government. The move to European monetary integration had been accompanied by a ban on the monetizing of public debt by the European Central Bank, as well as a no-bailout clause. The fiscal rules that were at the core of the Maastricht Treaty on monetary unification—limiting deficits to 3 percent of GDP and public debt to 60 percent—were intended to deal with a Europe in which there were very different levels of fiscal performance. In a crisis that requires Keynesian counter-cyclical measures, these rules might be discarded. But the still very divergent fiscal stances mean that Keynesian-style answers are only possible in a limited number of nation-states. France and Germany could afford them, while Greece, Italy, and Portugal could not. Between these extremes lay countries such as Spain and Ireland, whose fiscal performance before the outbreak of the crisis had been solid, but whose fiscal solutions to bank and indebtedness problems created a sudden spike in public-sector deficits. When Ireland started to rescue banks, the cost drove its fiscal balance from a surplus of almost 3 percent of GDP in 2006 to a projected deficit of over 11 percent for 2009. Outside the Eurozone, the same arithmetic concerning the public assumption of previously privately held debt also hit the United Kingdom. Furthermore, Europeans are worried that the effects of stimulus measures would simply spill over to other countries, leaving increased long-term burdens for the taxpayer. The decision-making of European states is paralyzed in the face of alternatives that do not look practicable: either concentrating more on a European-level fiscal stimulus (for which there is no political will); or taking measures to ensure that fiscal stimuli benefit national economies (which would be counter to the fundamental orientation of the European Union as an integrated market).

Third, pressures to reduce levels of migration have

increased. As with the rapid trade contraction of 2008–2009, by no means has all the reduction in global interconnectedness been the outcome of policy choices. Migrants return home in economic crises, and even the rate of internal migration in large countries such as the United States or China contracted dramatically after 2008. But the decline also reflects a turn in sentiment. In Britain and Germany, opinion surveys indicate majorities that oppose the movement of foreign nationals (including those from other European Union countries) in search of work.[19] Riots and protests against foreign workers erupted very soon after the deepening of the financial crisis in Britain, one of the most open economies in terms of its labor markets. Policymakers responded to such pressures with increased obstacles to migration, and in some countries such as Australia, with a lowering of immigration quotas. In the United States, banks taking government funds as part of a rescue package found that they were prevented from hiring foreign employees.

As eastern and central European members of the EU, who were still outside the Eurozone, faced a mixed banking and currency crisis of the 1931 type, and as employment contracted rapidly, there was a fear that labor driven out by the financial crisis would surge into the richer countries and impose new burdens on already strained social security systems. By the beginning of 2009, even some politicians in the old core countries of the EU began to argue pragmatically that EU members could not simply stand by and let a member country default.

Financial rescues in the modern globalization era have often been driven by the fear of the migration and labor market consequences of collapse. But usually such consequences have been limited in scope. France has long pressed international financial institutions to support Algeria for fear of a surge of Algerian immigrants. In 1997, Italian experts rushed to Albania to reconstruct, at substantial expense, the Albanian financial system after it had collapsed in the aftermath of a vast pyramid swindle. Two thousand people were killed in the subsequent rioting, and the Italian government feared that there would be a mass emigration to Italy.[20] The prompt and very expensive response of the United States to the 1994–1995 Mexico crisis, which was often called "the first financial crisis of the twenty-first century," was driven by worries about Mexicans surging across the southern border of the United States.

Because of its universal character, the financial crisis of 2008 threatens a much wider range of emerging markets than did the more isolated eruptions of the 1990s. Prosperous countries, worried about likely crisis-induced flows of migration, are thus demanding a more thorough and coordinated response to stem the most recent collapse. But although all the classic mechanisms of the globalization backlash are in place in the financial, goods, and labor markets, those mechanisms that might contain them have proven increasingly ineffective.

INTERNATIONAL INSTITUTIONS

Many political scientists believe that as an accompaniment of globalization, a new international or universal political regime was being created "after hegemony" that locked in a broad range of institutional commitments.[21] But those international institutions that were often held to constitute a strong framework for the globalization of the late twentieth century appeared exhausted and faltering at the outset of the new millennium.

At the end of the Second World War, and in response to the traumas of the Great Depression, two parallel sets of institutional safeguards had been envisaged: an International Trade Organization (ITO), to avoid the escalation of trade conflicts that occurred in the 1930s, and the International Monetary Fund (IMF), to provide a framework of monetary stability and cooperation. The ITO was never realized in its original form, because the United States rejected the demands for exemptions that came from almost every other would-be member country; but an alternative bargaining mechanism, the General Agreement on Tariffs and Trade (GATT), produced successive rounds of tariff reductions before its final round (the Uruguay round) established the World Trade Organization (WTO) in 1995.

During the late 1990s, both the WTO and IMF were the focus of intense political campaigns against globalization. The Seattle WTO meeting was the scene of violent protests. The IMF was widely attacked for imposing the interests of Wall Street and the U.S. Treasury Department on the Asian countries stricken by the Asian financial crisis of 1997–1998. But early in the next century, as the globalization debate subsided, the operations of both the WTO and the IMF became less of a target of protest. Both became much more marginal than they had been during the late twentieth-century process of opening up the world economy.

The WTO Doha round was sputtering even before the eruption of the financial crisis. Large developing countries argued that previous liberalizations had given too many concessions to industrial countries, especially in regard to access to markets in services. In trade politics, the United States and the European Union were turning to a self-consciously second-best option of bilateral trade agreements, and these were almost entirely with small and relatively insignificant economies. The immediate response of many countries to the financial crisis in 2008 was an increase in specifically targeted subsidies, which were harder to treat as trade issues at the WTO than old-style tariff or quota measures (which are controlled under WTO agreements). They are in fact better treated as elements of a global competition policy, which only in part comes under the auspices of the WTO.

When the twenty-first century began, after more than sixty years of existence—years in which there have been numerous ups and downs—the IMF was the focus of less conflict about its role and importance in the world economy. This was largely because the IMF has been almost completely sidelined from many of the major governance issues of the international financial system. Its financial activity fell away, leading economists like Benn Steil and Robert Litan to write about the "existential crisis of the Fund."[22] Is there any need for an institution such as the IMF?

The original mandate of the International Monetary Fund, as laid down in the 1944 Bretton Woods Articles of Agreement, was very general: to promote international monetary cooperation, facilitate the growth of world trade, promote exchange-rate stability, and help create a multilateral system of payments. In order to achieve these objectives, the fund was supposed to provide short-term balance-of-payments support to countries in need of additional reserves. The best way of thinking about the IMF's functions during the early period, the so-called Bretton Woods era (1945–1973), is not so much as a bureaucratic institution, but rather as the embodiment of a system of rules as laid out in the Articles of Agreement. But in the early 1970s the core of the rule-based system, the requirement that member countries adopt a par value, disappeared.

The IMF's evolution since the 1970s has reflected both the demand for its services in the light of new and perceived market failures and its willingness to provide those services. There has been a fundamental change of environment, characterized by the breakdown of the par value system, a new mobility of capital, and financial deregulation. Capital flows have taken a role that no one expected when the IMF was created. The international political system has changed too: the Soviet bloc collapsed economically and politically, and there are many new countries, with novel problems to solve.

The IMF developed in response to these external challenges. Those policies considered part of the surveillance exercise were expanded in scope. The number and duration of stabilization packages increased, even though they were only successful in a few cases. In the 1990s, in response to crises in a globalized capital market, the IMF engaged in liquidity crisis management. The new political environment of the 1990s led to an expansion into nonmacroeconomic policy areas, so that the IMF came to criticize military spending, corruption, and nondemocratic practices. After the Asian crises in 1997 and since, the IMF has also discussed areas such as corporate governance and accounting practices that traditionally lay outside its purview. A sign of the new orientation of the fund was the choice of chief economist: while until 2003 the chief economist had always been a distinguished macroeconomist, the next two chief economists were better known as microeconomists who specialize in improving corporate governance regimes.

The IMF's lending activities had fallen off after the resolution of the Argentine and Turkish financial collapses at the beginning of the new millennium. The virtual absence of lending (which produced income for the day-to-day activity of the fund) sparked a debate over whether the IMF could even survive. The fund engaged in a large-scale downsizing of its staff, and seemed to be preparing itself for a life of institutional somnolence. Once the 2008 crisis broke out, it was no longer emerging markets alone that required rescue operations, and the IMF suddenly and very dramatically looked short of loanable resources. In practice, solutions needed to be patched together, with swap lines from the Federal Reserve and from China and Japan, and with the involvement of the EU in a Hungarian and Latvian package. Attempts at crisis prevention by the IMF in the form of the creation of conditional facilities were problematic. Even before the crisis, some academics had proposed an insurance facility; but the new, easier-access Short Term Liquidity Facility launched in October 2008 was never used. (It was analogous to the also unused Contingent Credit Line Facility created in 1999 in the wake of the Asia crisis.) The London G-20 summit in April 2009 increased the funds available to the IMF, in part through commitments of countries to provide new lending, and in part through the issue of new synthetic money in the form of the IMF's currency, Special Drawing Rights (SDRs).

On the most tense monetary issue of the previous years, the question of whether the Chinese-controlled exchange rate of the renminbi was appropriate, or whether it constituted a form of protectionism or mercantilism as many American and other critics alleged, the IMF was frustratingly silent in the lead-up to, as well as during, the crisis.[23] In the 1990s, in dealing with the Asia crisis, accusations flew that the IMF was doing too much, and extending itself far beyond its area of competence. It responded to that criticism by retreating to a shell. The new engagement of the IMF is linked to a discussion of governance reform, and in particular of improved representation for the emerging markets. Reform negotiations are inevitably complex and protracted, but it is likely that China in particular will want to play a stronger part than before and would be unhappy with continued U.S. domination of international institutions.

An alternative forum for monetary discussion, and

specifically for central bank cooperation, is the Bank for International Settlements (BIS), which originated during the depression era. From the 1980s, it was actively engaged in debates about global financial regulation.[24] But in 2004 the experts meeting in Basel concluded a set of agreements on capital adequacy (Basel II) that introduced a strongly procyclical element: with an expansion of credit, and an apparent reduction of risk, the risk-weighting went down. Consequently, the pillars of the Basel agreement allowed an effective reduction of the capital base. Indeed the agreement explicitly recognized the problem: "it may be costly for banks to raise additional capital, especially if this needs to be done quickly or at a time when market conditions are unfavourable" (paragraph 757c). While annual reports from the BIS warned about this possible problem in increasingly dramatic terms, these warnings did not impress anyone (at least anyone who mattered). Consequently, when the 2008 financial credit crisis hit and there was an immediate renewed interest in the adequate capitalization of banks, the easiest way to strengthen the balance sheet of banks lay not in access to new capital, but in a reduction of lending, a solution that has had a clearly negative macroeconomic impact.

In March 2009, the existing Financial Stability Forum was tweaked slightly to make it into the Financial Stability Board, with an implicit expansion of its reach. The calls for effective early warning systems and for better surveillance, which had been made repeatedly in response to earlier crises, were also repeated.

A crisis of global governance affects both the private and the public sectors. As was the case in the Great Depression, a great deal of crisis diplomacy took place. Both then and now, financial collapse leads to more—and more urgent—meetings. Some of the financial statesmen in the 1931 crisis used the new means of transportation—especially the aeroplane— to engage in shuttle diplomacy. The World Economic Conference that met in the Kensington Geological Museum in London in June 1933 was the largest gathering for an economic conference in human history. Its size did not make it more effective.

The year 2008 also produced increasingly breathless rounds of international financial diplomacy, which may have had little to do with the financial crisis: in the second half of the year, France took its turn at leading the European Union, and France's president, Nicolas Sarkozy, in his drive to exercise a European influence on the global stage, set about expanding France's and Europe's role with a hyperactive zeal. He squeezed out other representatives of the complex European system of governance—the president of the commission, the much quieter Portuguese politician José Manuel Barroso; as well as the veteran president of the Eurogroup of Finance Ministers, the Luxembourger Jean-Claude Juncker. He inundated the international diplomatic pipelines with proposals for a new Bretton Woods, although it was not clear what such a new conference might produce. He also suggested a French national Sovereign Wealth Fund to buy endangered French assets and protect national industry.

The flood of new French initiatives inspired the other big countries of the European Union to parade their own solutions. The British prime minister's scheme for the rescue of British banks in September 2008 was widely praised, and he went on to suggest that it might be a basis on which to "rescue the world." German chancellor Angela Merkel, faced with an increasingly rancorous and unsettled domestic coalition, in which both the right and the left wings were chafing, suggested that the world should have an economic council that would parallel the United Nations Security Council. A committee of economists convoked by President Sarkozy reached a similar conclusion.

All these suggestions, by heads of government or state, seemed to build on the idea that the finance ministers and central bankers had not successfully dealt with the problems. In trying to move discussions up to the highest political level, the new proposals replicated discussions of the 1970s, when the Group of Five Finance Ministers meeting was succeeded by the G-5 meeting of the heads of state of the United States, the United Kingdom, France, Germany, and Japan—a meeting that continues today, even though it is now usually characterized by nothing more important than the routine exchange of platitudes. By the 2008 crisis, the G-5 had become the G-8 (with the addition of Canada, Italy, and in the 1990s, post-Soviet Russia) but still was obviously unrepresentative. In particular, the large emerging market economies, which have the major surpluses, were unrepresented. Thus Gordon Brown and others advocated for a G-20 as a more appropriate forum for reform discussions. This newer governance entity met in Washington in November 2008, and produced a declaration urging a continued commitment to global openness. But soon afterward, several of the participants imposed new restrictions on trade, including tariffs on automobiles in Russia and on steel products in India. In fact, the idea that really high-level policy reform can be made more effectively by dramatic high-level political meetings than in routine cooperation between large numbers of officials has been challenged by the outcome of the G-20 meeting. While it produced some results, above all in regard to IMF funding and trade finance, it did not revolutionize international governance. The most prominent of the promised results, a commitment to coordinated global fiscal stimulus, was not realized. Choice about stimulus measures was left to the individual countries.

The failure of political internationalism and problems related to financial interconnectedness have pushed the world back into dependence on the power and effectiveness of governments. But are these governments up to the task? George Soros, for one, has long complained that there exist fewer and fewer common values that bind a society together, and that there has been a "general failure of politics both on the national and the international level."[25] Certainly the increased demands strain the political process. In practice, only very large states can really take on the new role. U.S. policymakers are treating a new state capitalism as the emerging global reality. In continental Europe, politicians find it attractive to suggest that capitalism (which they usually identify with a so-called Anglo-Saxon model of financially driven globalization) has been discredited. President Sarkozy has promoted "the return of politics," meaning a much more active role for the state in nationalizing strategic industries to prevent them from falling under foreign control. The German finance minister, Peer Steinbrück, has suggested that Karl Marx was "not all that incorrect" in his analysis of the periodically crisis-prone character of capitalism. A German filmmaker is even proposing to make a movie of *Das Kapital*. The state is needed, according to this argument, because the previous framing vision of financially driven globalization has disintegrated.

4

THE EXTENT AND LIMIT OF THE
FINANCIAL REVOLUTION

THE RECENT EPISODE of globalization was driven by a dramatic expansion of financial flows. Looking at the experience of some successful emerging market economies, notably Chile and some small East Asian economies, the economist and former Federal Reserve governor Frederic Mishkin asserted that "these countries prove that the next great globalization should be financial."[1] There is nothing wrong with the assertion except its tense. In 2009 we can already say that the *last* great globalization *was* financial.

The disintegration of financial globalization has produced an intellectual crisis for economists who had been gripped by the idea of market perfectibility and rational foresight. Roman Frydman and Michael Goldberg warned in 2007 (in the context of a discussion of exchange rates) that "causal relationships in economics are temporally unstable in ways and at times that no one can fully foresee."[2] But many of the attempts to formulate alternative perspectives lacked intellectual foundation or academic gravitas. In the early stages of the contemporary crisis, George Soros argued that economists were as responsible as investment bankers for the excessive faith in rational expectations models, and demanded that the economists also pay a price for their mistakes: "Economists," he said, "have to accept a reduction of their status."[3] Some analysts may have foreseen the crisis, but more on the basis of a gut feeling about instability than because of a precisely formulated analysis of complex connections, which remained necessarily obscure.

The scale and reach of the financial revolution were broad enough to instill the widespread perception that this was a phenomenon that had created new realities. Whereas net financial flows were not dissimilar to those of the pre-1914 globalization era, the extent of the gross flows is remarkable and has no historical parallel. This financial explosion can also be described as a buildup of debt, both on a global and a personal level. In the United States, debt in 1980 amounted to 163 percent of GDP, but by 2007 the figure was 346 percent. Household debt increased from 50 to 100 percent of GDP, while the liabilities of the financial sector increased much faster, from 21 percent to 116 percent.

Domestic debt presents its own problems, but a good deal of the debt was traded across national frontiers. International banking transactions grew, not slowly and surely, but erratically. The expansion of cross-national lending was particularly explosive during the last years of the growth era, after 2005. Regulation, however, remained primarily national, even in such a well-integrated capital and money market as the Eurozone, despite repeated efforts to harness, mold, or manage the course of financial globalization.[4] After the outbreak of the crisis, some influential analysts, such as Adair Turner, the chairman of Britain's Financial Services Authority, argued that the demand for enhanced regulation should be met at the international level, but if that were impossible, more domestic action was required as a second-best option.[5]

The rapid growth of international claims, with their implied vulnerability, makes the growth period look like a classical credit boom. As with other booms, such as the international lending surge of the 1920s,

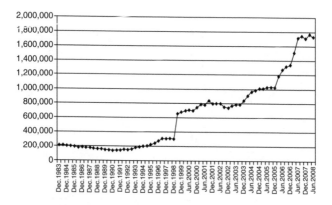

Foreign claims of U.S. banks, 1983–2008 (in thousand dollars).

Source: Bank for International Settlements.

there was a deterioration in credit during the last
phases of expansion.[6] For subprime lending, the pattern of deterioration is especially clear. When mortgage delinquencies are separated by their year of issue, credits given in 2003 and 2004 look better than
those of 2000, while 2005 is worse for subprime and
the next lowest grade, Alt-A, and 2006 and 2007 are
even more radically deteriorated. By contrast, for
prime mortgages, the same effect is not visible, and
only the 2007 mortgages performed worse than those
from 2000.[7]

Financial stocks relative to general index, 1992–2008. 1992 = 100.

Source: Global Financial Data.

In 2005 and 2006 the world was gripped by a new certainty that globalization was back after the dot-com collapse of 2000–2001 and the geopolitical challenges of 2001–2003. Most believed that the new environment was stable. Really. There was a delusional calm before the storm.

The explosion of debt could be viewed in a calm way because of two soothing considerations. First, it was reassuring that the debt was constantly traded because it had been securitized. The concept of securitization is quite old: joint stock companies, for instance, constitute a form of securitization, in that a paper (or now electronic) claim is created to be a part of the company's revenue stream. Bonds, traded instruments of a company or a government's debts, are securities. They are relatively simple forms of securitization, in which the relationship of the underlying entity to the traded paper is relatively clear. The fundamental advantage of securities is that they offer the possibility of acquiring exposure to risk in small, almost risk-free increments. The modern investor does not need to behave like Shakespeare's merchant of Venice and place his fortune all on one ship or one fleet.

The principle of distributing risk had been developed into an increasingly rarified discipline. At the outset of the modern age of financial globalization there emerged the idea that not only sophisticated but even everyday investors could minimize their risk by investing in a wide array of funds. In the middle of the 1970s, Paul Samuelson posed a "Challenge to Judgment," in which the key principle was to increase exposure to as broad a range of investments as possible. In 1976 John Bogle launched the first stock index fund.[8]

The most recent fundamental innovation of securitization is usually dated to the middle of the 1990s, and associated with J. P. Morgan.[9] The decisive innovation was the Broad Index Securitized Trust Offering (BISTRO). First launched in 1997, it broke credit exposure into sections or tranches, and transferred them to another legal entity, which might be simply an off-balance-sheet unit run by the issuing bank called a Structured Investment Vehicle (SIV). The genius of the modern version of securitization is that very different debt relations were reduced to a common form that could then be traded in ever more complex transactions. It is analogous to the introduction in the nineteenth century of a common measure of grain quality, so that the commodity could be traded in bulk without an inspector having to scrutinize handfuls of the product at each step of the exchange. The quality could be simply certified at one particular trading post and then be taken for granted.

The financial innovations were widely celebrated as transforming the prospects for the American economy. In a speech given in the immediate aftermath of the collapse of the hedge fund Long-Term Capital

Management (LTCM), when big doubts had sprung up about the instability of the new world of finance, Alan Greenspan said:

> Dramatic advances in computer and telecommunications technologies in recent years have enabled a broad unbundling of risks through innovative financial engineering. The financial instruments of a bygone era, common stocks and debt obligations, have been augmented by a vast array of complex hybrid financial products, which allow risks to be isolated, but which, in many cases, seemingly challenge human understanding. The consequence doubtless has been a far more efficient financial system. The price-setting functions of the market economy in the United States, for example, have become increasingly sensitive to subtle changes in consumer choice and capital efficiencies, and the resulting set of product and asset market prices and interest rates have enabled producers to direct scarce capital to those productive facilities that most effectively cater to consumer preferences. Thus, despite a rate of capital investment far short of that of many other advanced industrial countries, the efficiency of that capital has facilitated

the creation of an economy whose vitality is un-
matched throughout the world.[10]

By the start of the new century, securitization had
transformed the real estate business. The first securitization of subprime debt was underwritten in 1997
by Bear Stearns and First Union Capital Markets.
There was a certification process in subprime mortgage debt, but the certifier bore no responsibility for
what subsequently happened to the credit. After certification, the overwhelming majority of subprime
mortgages (an estimated 80 or 90 percent) were repackaged into pools, and the securities split up according to their likelihood of default. The same
mortgage could thus in the course of the repackag-
ing find itself in several pools, each of which consisted of thousands of mortgages. Since it was unlikely that there would be a complete default on any
mortgage, and the calculation was that something
would always be recoverable, the upper sections (or
"tranches") of even a very bad mortgage looked like
solid investment material. The results of the pool-
ing could then be validated in a different way, by a
credit-rating agency, and the best tranche had a very
good grade. Over the period 2005–2007, some $540
billion of collateralized debt obligations and asset-

backed securities were created. By early 2009, $102 billion of these had been liquidated, with recovery rates of only 32 percent for the highest-rated (AAA) products and 5 percent for less well rated (mezzanine) products.[11]

Such standardization allowed a large increase in the mortgage business. The beneficial result, that many more people owned their homes, was widely heralded as a great social achievement, a sort of private-sector victory equivalent to the Great Society welfare programs of the 1960s. There was a great political welcome for the transformative magic of finance; the new developments attracted bipartisan consensus and seemed to be an extension of the American promise and the American dream. White House initiatives had bolstered the appeal of home ownership for all: the Clinton administration in 1995 had strengthened the 1977 Community Reinvestment Act to give banks ratings on the basis of their lending in low-income neighborhoods; and in 2003 the Bush administration provided payments to cover closing costs and down payments for first-time, low-income house buyers.

The new sophistication of the U.S. financial market also attracted new inflows of money to instruments that were apparently transparent and reliable.

Financial innovation was thus one of the drivers of the expansion of capital flows into the United States, as the U.S. financial system distributed its bright new products around the world. Securities had become a standardized product for which deep and liquid markets existed.

The second innovation is that the securities could be insured through the issuance of further securities. In the process of separating different properties of a credit, the risk of default could be separated from the other attributes. In consequence, any security could in theory be bought in a default-free form, meaning that for the purchaser, there would be no risk. It was also possible for insurers to pass on the risk via new insurance contracts, so that the likelihood of being hit in the event of a default would be small. Credit default swaps, another J. P. Morgan securitization innovation of 1995, in 2008 accounted for $58 trillion, in other words more than the world's GDP ($50 trillion). It was the market for these swaps that was endangered by the collapse of Lehman Brothers in September 2008, and its paralysis has since spread to almost every kind of economic activity: to the market for corporate debt, to trade finance, and hence to commerce and production.

In particular, large and diversified insurance groups

such as AIG International and Swiss Re found it attractive to issue these insurances, because they produced a reliable fee income with apparently very little risk exposure.

Regulators wanted to ensure that banks managed their risks correctly, and encouraged financial institutions to distribute and insure their risk. The apparently risk-free properties of debt were thus a creation of regulatory agencies that rightly wanted to minimize the vulnerability of the financial system. In the five years that followed 2003, the ten largest publicly listed banks in Europe and the United States doubled their aggregate assets, to €15 trillion, but the rise in risk-weighted assets, which was used to calculate the capital adequacy ratios required by regulators, only amounted to €5 trillion. Risk-adjusted capital adequacy ratios required by regulators thus became effectively meaningless. In fact the capital adequacy ratios of banks that subsequently turned out to require government intervention in the credit crisis were stronger than those of banks that did not require intervention.[12]

Some additional factors might have set off the dramatic credit boom, particularly its explosive final phase after 2005. In 2005 changes in bankruptcy laws made disorderly bankruptcy easier. The intention of

the new rule had been to insulate financial companies from the collapse of a large counterparty such
as a hedge fund. It exempted a range of securities
including credit default swaps and mortgage repur-
chase agreements from standard bankruptcy proce-
dures. In practice, however, the removal of bankruptcy
protection made it easier to close down positions
quickly.[13]

A critical role was also played by the development
of off-balance-sheet units controlled by banks, and
by the parent banks' practice of borrowing on the security of repackaged financial instruments. The language of bank annual reports of this era became very
curious. They customarily stated "we are involved
with . . . ," leaving the nature of the involvement
seeming rather shady and implying that there was no
contractual obligation to meet the obligations of the
new investment vehicles. Indeed, in private life the
phrase "I am involved with . . ." still often carries a
tinge of the improper. In practice, in 2007, as values
began to collapse, some of the major banks had to
act promptly to rescue their investment vehicles.

The most obvious culprit for the credit boom, however, is the Federal Reserve System's policy of rapid
interest-rate cuts in order to deal with the recession

of 2001, combined with its reluctance to begin tightening interest rates.

Like previous globalization eras, the recent past was characterized by a fast pace of innovation. Its results produced a great deal of relatively widely dispersed global wealth and well-being, with the conquest of global poverty looking more feasible at the beginning of the twenty-first century than at any previous moment. The pace of innovation looked miraculous, and the major figure behind the development of securitization at J. P. Morgan, Blythe Masters, is supposed to have referred to her achievement as "offering the financial equivalent of a free lunch."[14] But there may have been too much innovation to digest.

PREVIOUS TRANSITIONS

Previous globalizations were also characterized by the special dynamism of one sector of the economy. Eighteenth-century expansion was driven by big productivity increases in agriculture, which led to increased purchasing power and made possible a consumer revolution during the so-called First Industrial Revolution. And during the second half of the nineteenth century, a transformative global expansion of manufacturing, especially in iron and steel, engineered a transportation revolution that led to, among other innovations, the steam engine, the railroad, and the iron-hulled steamship.

Economic historians consequently identify two big shifts in activity and employment over the past two hundred years: the transition from agriculture to manufacturing during the nineteenth century, and a move away from the "old" manufacturing into services during the twentieth. But in each case, a dramatic crisis created the conditions for change. The last big hunger crisis of traditional rural Europe occurred in the 1840s, with crop failures over most of the continent leading to inadequate food supplies and starvation. It was the miserable experience of global integration, and its transformative but disruptive effects, that provided the background to Karl Marx and Friedrich Engels's analysis in *The Communist Manifesto*, written in the crisis year 1848:

> The bourgeoisie has through its exploitation of the world-market given a cosmopolitan character to production and consumption in every country . . . it has drawn from under the feet of industry the national ground on which it stood. All old-established national industries have been

> destroyed or are daily being destroyed. . . . Na-
> tional differences and antagonisms between
> peoples are daily more and more vanishing, ow-
> ing to the development of the bourgeoisie, to
> freedom of commerce, to the world-market, to
> uniformity in the mode of production and in
> the conditions of life corresponding thereto.[15]

The impoverishment of agriculture was sufficient to produce a major downturn for everyone else. When the crisis was over, many farmers moved to other activities, and a major boom in the core businesses of the First Industrial Revolution began.

Like the agrarian crisis of the 1840s, the Great Depression of the 1930s transformed economic structures. In the short run it looked devastating, and governments contemplated as many measures as they could for increasing manufacturing employment as a way to ease the strain. But widespread industrial unemployment eventually pushed workers into new occupations, and underlined the importance of the skills and education that proved vital for the development of the service economy of the late twentieth century. A long-term and beneficial legacy of the grim experience of the depression years was the widespread conviction that an increase in skills offered a way out of misery. Every major industrial country started to invest large amounts in the expansion of high schools and universities, and such enhanced skill levels boosted productivity and reduced inequality.[16] Industry as a share of output in the major industrial economies reached its height in the middle of the twentieth century: in Sweden and the Netherlands in 1950, in the United Kingdom and France in 1951, and in the United States in 1953. (Germany's record is dislocated by the Nazi rearmament program and by the postwar division, but West Germany never reached the share of industry in total output that it had had in the interwar period, and its peacetime highwater mark is 1937.[17])

During each economic and employment transition, the older businesses did not stop. They just learned to operate more efficiently. Innovation did not come to an end. With a tiny farm population, the United States as the world's largest economy still continues as a major agricultural producer and exporter. And despite all the discussion of deindustrialization and loss of relative competitiveness since the 1970s and 1980s, the United States is also still (just barely) the world's largest manufacturer.

The movement of the twentieth century into services can be broken into two phases. First, and in large part as a response to the Great Depression, as well as to the Second World War, all industrial countries saw a massive growth in government employment. The enthusiasm for state-run economies reached a peak in the 1970s, with the widespread realization that the public sector simply could not go on growing. Electoral pressures produced a new emphasis on efficiency in the provision of public services. Privatization became the obvious source of efficiency, and required a new approach to the financing of public goods. Secondly, then, a new sort of economic growth set in. From the 1970s, the breaking down of national frontiers helped to promote financial globalization and with it an explosive growth in the demand for financial services.

WHAT HAPPENS IN PREVIOUSLY DYNAMIC SECTORS?

The credit crunch of 2007–2008 is a turning point because it has revealed some serious weaknesses in the growth sector of the past decades. It was precisely in the world's most financially sophisticated countries, the United States, the United Kingdom, France, Germany, and Switzerland, that the flaws in bank supervision became most apparent. By contrast, Canada,

Italy, and Spain, which had dynamic banking systems but were widely regarded as rather sleepy, had much better and tighter supervision. Japanese banks were also not as centrally affected: they had been so battered by the dismal experience of the 1990s that they had not had the chance to experiment in the new world of finance.

The financial-sector flaws were not just in the area of external supervision; internal risk management in financial institutions was also frequently inadequate. Directors of risk management who warned against the general line of aggressively expansionist policy were sidelined or dismissed. Paul Moore, the group head of regulatory risk at HBOS, was sacked in late 2004 for being too cautious. He later told a parliamentary committee in the United Kingdom: "This crisis was caused not because many bright people did not see it coming but because there has been a completely inadequate separation and balance of power between the executive and all those accounting for their actions and reining them in, i.e. internal control functions such as finance, risk, compliance and internal audit, non-executive chairmen and directors, external auditors, the FSA [Financial Services Authority], shareholders and politicians."[18]

By 2008, however, there was a new mood of sobriety. In June 2008, just before the implosion, Lehman Brothers dismissed its chief financial officer, Erin Callan. A 2008 inquiry into the woes of the Swiss bank UBS stated that "the overall Risk Control framework was insufficiently robust," and that there had been a "failure to demand a holistic risk assessment."[19]

In the new view generated with the benefit of hindsight, a particular focus of attention was the use of chronologically limited sets of data, often from a period as small as five years, to generate scenarios for different possibilities of risk.

It was the smaller, less-regulated financial centers that were most vulnerable. The most dramatic crisis of 2008 broke out in Iceland in early October. Its three largest banks had had a dramatic expansion over the previous five years. In mid-2006, they had been shocked by a mini-crisis, which they had dealt with by restructuring and by attempting to cut their problematic exposure. By September 2008, most observers thought they were sounder than they had been a few years earlier, but that month, the Icelandic central bank, faced by a liquidity strain, refused a short-term credit to Glitnir, the most vulnerable of the beleaguered banks, and insisted on its full-scale nationalization. This measure led to margin calls on the other Icelandic banks. The prime minister's nationalistic rhetoric about the responsibility of speculative and foreign (largely British) depositors fanned the panic. In consequence, there was a simultaneous bank crisis, currency crisis as the krona depreciated rapidly, and crisis of the government budget, which could not meet the strain of the costs of bank nationalization. In short this was a reappearance of the same triangle of bank, currency, and fiscal crisis that had characterized the meltdown of 1931.

In facing the crisis, Iceland's prime minister felt abandoned by the international community and in a bold geopolitical gamble turned to Russia for support. He explained, "We have not received the kind of support that we were requiring from our friends. So in a situation like that one has to look for new friends."[20] But the collapse of the banks turned into a new geopolitical fiasco, with Britain using extraordinary measures intended to counter the financing of terrorism in order to seize Icelandic assets.

Mishkin has argued that lending booms and crashes are not inevitable outcomes of financial liberalization and globalization, despite appearances, and that "they occur only when there is an institutional weakness that prevents the nation from successfully handling the liberalization/globalization process."[21]

It turns out that institutional weakness was so prevalent as to be nearly ubiquitous, and that Iceland was merely an extreme example of a much wider problem.

How will current institutions adapt to the trauma of the financial crisis? A conventional response to financial disorder is a demand for more regulation. Governments are also moving to take direct or indirect ownership of banks, with a compulsory recapitalization of U.S. and French financial institutions. In 2008, around 70 percent of European bank mergers and acquisitions involved government acquisitions. There is, however, a great deal of historical evidence, not only from emerging markets but also from industrial countries with a large publicly owned banking sector, that it is the publicly owned banks that accumulate risk disproportionately. It was the German publicly owned Landesbanken that experienced the greatest losses in the 1997 Asia crisis, and ran into difficulty in 2007 because of its exposure to U.S. subprime lending. State-owned banks in Indonesia and Turkey were at the heart of the financial problems of those countries in the 1990s and 2000s.[22]

The private-sector banks that experienced problems and were exposed in 2007 and 2008 had unduly concentrated risk in large institutions; but public-sector agglomerations of risk pose an even greater danger of concentration, in addition to the new element of danger stemming from politically directed lending. Government ownership and increased government supervision are likely to influence the character of future lending operations. In particular, the change produces pressure to cut back international lending and to direct credit to those sectors of the economy that are believed to be economically or politically important. Where banks' participation in a government assistance program was voluntary, it was often resisted exactly for this reason. For example, in Italy, the first bank to participate in the government recapitalization program, Banco Popular, was subject to a very detailed regional level supervision of its lending practices, and the other banks treated the program as a political intrusion that should be avoided if at all possible.

There are analogies for the extension of regulation of a fast-growing but problematic sector in the previous waves of economic development. Faced by agricultural distress, well-intentioned people in the 1840s called for a greater regulation of agricultural prices. In the industrial chaos of the 1930s, forced amalgamations, cartels, and state supervision seemed like a good answer.

The statements of today echo precisely the sentiments of that apparently distant epoch. The British prime minister, Gordon Brown, stated in 2009: "We want to ensure that the new banking system that emerges over the coming years meets all these requirements—and becomes the servant of our economy and society, never its master."[23] Similarly, in 1931, the German finance minister, Hermann Dietrich, told his cabinet colleagues: "The banks should support the economy. But instead they wanted to dominate it, and for this reason constructed complicated business structures. But they could not deal with them. The banks will turn their situation into the opposite of what they want if they keep on with today's demands. The accumulation of risk premia has led to the most severe collapses."[24] Each of these comments not only recognizes the political urgency of focusing on government control during a banking crisis, but also hints at another important truth: regulation is relatively simple to achieve in national financial markets, but much more difficult to accomplish when complex cross-border issues are involved.

Some of the new style of financial life will lie in a simplification, a movement back to basics, or in what Amar Bhidé calls "retro finance."[25] There may be regulatory requirements to stop the emergence of new large and complex institutions that are "too big to fail." Europeans and Asians remember savings banks as institutions in which small or large personal savings were really safe (except from the ravages of inflation). The longtime Japanese vice minister of finance, Eisuke Sakakibara, as "Mr. Yen," now argues that the old Japan, isolated from the world, was peaceful, orderly, unspoiled, and friendly. "That was what pre-Meiji Japan was like. We should go back to that."[26] For some time, most investors are likely—even without new regulatory intervention—to avoid very sophisticated financial products. But multiplying face-to-face encounters and subjective judgments while reducing standardized credit scoring also increases the potential for arbitrariness and erroneous or corrupt assessments. The development of financial services is more likely to move in a similar direction to that of innovative economic sectors in the past. It is unlikely that the technical processes of slicing debt will simply be abandoned, but they will need to become more transparent.

The better answers to the perils of excessive growth and innovation have always lain paradoxically in further technical change. Raising productivity in agriculture or industry through the use of new techniques and new equipment meant that these activities could become much more productive, while employing fewer people and generating less macro-economic vulnerability. The interaction of millions of participants in the operation of a market allows the gains produced by the application of new technology to be diffused widely as productivity gains, and thus also as increases in income.

Innovation is likely to be the long-run answer to banking problems as well. In particular, regulatory and supervisory functions will be handled—as they have been in the wake of the credit crunch—by an intensified testing of responses to hypothetical situations (the failure of a big counterparty; a geopolitical upheaval and so on).

It is also possible to imagine the development over the longer term of some technical alternatives that will make finance more transparent, and thus less prone to the asymmetric information issues—issues that require a high level of confidence on the part of depositors and investors to reduce a perpetual likelihood of panic and crisis.

An analogy might help to illustrate the direction of future developments. A conventional book contains many assertions that may be difficult to verify. In a very academic book, some, many, or even most of the assertions and factual statements will be carefully footnoted. But the reader of even an extensively documented book will often not bother to do the checking, and may be convinced by the simple lineup of apparently authoritative citations. Even if a really attentive reader does want to follow up, the books referred to may be in remote libraries or inaccessible archives. A modern approach, however, could present references as hyperlinks, so that a simple click would lead the reader to the source of the assertion, then to other sources, and so on. Some texts already have moved in this direction. There exist, in short, electronic ways of picking complexity apart, and of showing the inner structure of complicated constructs.

Are such innovations applicable to financial strategy? The traditional feature of a bank is precisely that it is a black box. The bank knows more about where its money goes than do its depositors or creditors. Investment banks gave advice to corporations on mergers and acquisitions, but also issued securities and did their own proprietary trading. Each of the counterparties in these transactions assumed that they were getting something special from the accumulated insights that the bank had acquired from its other branches of business, insights that derive fundamentally from permanent conflicts of interest. The activities were separated by so-called Chinese walls within the firm, but in practice the market participants assumed some leakage of information through the walls. The genius of the innovation of the 1990s was that it in theory allowed the bypassing of banks because securities took the place of traditional bank credits. But in the way the banks actually used that innovation, they placed transparent securities in nontransparent investment vehicles to which they then lent money. The black box character of banks is the source of their vulnerability.

In the major scandals that emerged in 2008–2009, of Bernard Madoff or Allen Stanford, individuals entrusted their money to financiers who cultivated some external confidence-building characteristic—such as an interest in philanthropy or cricket— as a substitute for insight into a nontransparent operation. It seems preferable to look for a more systematic or fool- and knave-proof way in which institutions and managers can demonstrate their competence and reliability. An analogy to the hyperlinked text would be that institutions and their regulators, but also their investors, might be able to see precisely what assets are being bought, what those assets relate to, and so forth. They would no longer be dealing with disembodied abstractions.

Conflict-of-interest situations might be handled by algorithms that authorize or prohibit transactions.

In the same way as trading floors are now mostly obsolete, and payment mechanisms have been automated, many other banking functions can and will be handled by machines rather than by error-prone humans. Financial intermediation will become simply an interaction of software systems.

As in previous transition phases, the individuals who work in the industry will try to produce convincing arguments for why their business depends on the human touch. Harvesting machines were supposed to lower the quality of the grain collected, because it was no longer subject to immediate inspection by the human eye. Advanced automobile plants are now largely composed of collections of robots. For a long time, British train drivers insisted that two people were needed to ensure transportation safety. It took a long time to convince the public that one-man trains were safe, but by now, some mass transit systems are working with driverless trains. A personal banker is a status symbol, but nothing more, and certainly not a necessity.

The recent application of psychology to economics has led to a dramatic demonstration of the irrational basis of many human decisions. The story of the credit crunch has often featured familiar characters from much older financial crises—for instance, the flawed individual, the financial scoundrel, or the rogue trader. It was perfectly predictable that someone such as Bernie Madoff should emerge as the symbol of our new predicament, in just the same way as the Great Depression made and then broke the Swedish "match king" Ivar Kreuger.

Perhaps new technology will allow us to do better. The application of electronics would eliminate much of the potential for the errors and flaws of humans to create havoc. The "Monday morning car," the defective automobile produced by exhausted assembly-line workers after a busy weekend, no longer exists; neither should its equivalent in the financial world. Finance will no longer be our master. But that will only be the case if we know more about it than the insiders, and that requires both transparency and the spread of financial knowledge.

5

THE IMPORTANCE OF POWER
POLITICS

CRISES, ESPECIALLY SEVERE CRISES, have a purgative effect. In the business world, insolvent businesses that adopted a bad strategy close down, and bad loans are written off. Then lenders can lend with a new confidence again. This is the process that Joseph Schumpeter celebrated as creative destruction. The same sort of evolution through occasional catastrophe may occur not simply with business institutions, but also with political forms. When a systemic economic crisis erupts, there is a possibility that it will lead to the elimination of political institutions that lack legitimacy or cannot accommodate the new stresses and expectations. But more often, political institutions have a different pathology, and instead of fading away become maligned, dysfunctional, and aggressive.

Governments become more vulnerable when economies falter; in fact, the credibility of governments is often thought to be linked very closely to effective economic performance. In the early stages of the 2008 crisis, the governments of Belgium, Iceland, and Latvia fell. In 2009 the government of Kuwait dismissed the parliament after a dispute over the handling of the financial crisis. The Hungarian government collapsed in 2009 for similar reasons. So did that of the Czech Republic, leaving the (rotating) presidency of the European Union in chaos. There are many historic examples of government collapse in the wake of financial disaster, and it is actually hard to find counterexamples of governments that are so strong that they can withstand the consequences of such a meltdown.

The usual nature or direction of the political effects of crisis, however, is somewhat unpredictable. In some historical cases, regimes seem to be pushed to democratize, while in other circumstances, authoritarian answers to the crisis become more attractive.[1] An interesting and telling example, because it concerns the same country and the same leader, is the case of Italy in the interwar era. In the 1920s, a mild financial crisis made Benito Mussolini's government more compliant with the international order and more willing to halt exercises in imperial adventurism; in the 1930s, by contrast, the much greater severity and international dissemination of the international crisis reduced the rewards for good behavior, loosened the bounds that had kept political adventurers in check, and led to Mussolini's becoming ever more belligerent. In the 1930s, there was a clear association between the collapse of liberal economics and the weakness of liberal political regime. In many countries, the Great Depression prepared the way for authoritarian regimes and dictatorships.

Debt crises in Latin America during the 1980s, however, were often associated with democratization. High levels of debt, and the problem of servicing it, at least played some part in the collapse of communist authoritarianism in Hungary and Poland. The 1997 Asia crisis also launched a push for democratic change. The Suharto regime in Indonesia disintegrated. The Korean presidential elections, held at the height of the crisis, were won by Kim Dae-Jung, a long-standing critic of authoritarian government. Thailand adopted a new constitution in the wake of the crisis, and a new and popularly elected government under Chuan Leekpai managed the adjustment policies. There are efficiency arguments on both sides: autocracies can make decisions more easily, while democracies have the power to carry out deeper institutional reforms because of their greater legitimacy.

Crises can shape attitudes not only about the viability of democracy or autocracy, but also about the orientation of a country to the prevailing international order. A financial crisis may tip the balance of power between business interests that benefit from economic openness and those who prefer to make collective agreements in a closed-off national corporatism. In the 1980s and 1990s, the robustness of the global economic framework meant that on the whole the arguments in favor of increased integration, despite the costs of crisis, tended to win out. In generally expansive and optimistic times, openness promises that more resources can be made available from the outside.

Financial crises have, however, also lent themselves to the formulation of conspiracy theories. The political balance can easily swing against democracy and against openness, as a vision of mutually beneficial ("win-win") globalization is replaced by a zero-sum-game version, in which every gain corresponds to someone else's losses. The latter approach is usually accompanied by a rich vein of paranoia. The 1997–1998 crises were widely interpreted in Asia as the results of American intrigue. The same sort of criticism erupted in many crisis-hit countries in 2008 and 2009, where it derived additional force from the fact that the financial meltdown had so obviously originated in the United States. In Russia, Vladimir Putin has repeatedly emphasized the American origins of the crisis, and demanded that a new and alternative international architecture be created to resolve the problem. The argument is simple to make, and takes off from some elementary premises that follow from the stylized facts of previous rounds of financial disruption, notably the experience of the 1997 Asia crisis. These premises are first, that previous crises have tended to drive the world toward greater openness, liberalism, and international interconnectedness, and that markets have been freed in response to the damage caused by crisis; and second, that these developments have been to the advantage of the United States above all. It follows from these two assumptions that the United States may have an interest in promoting economic crisis, and it is only a matter of joining up the dots of a widely believed interpretation to misconstrue the crisis as an American-inspired one that has been carefully crafted to weaken the rest of the world.

When such a conspiratorial view gains hold, those who promote the advantages of economic openness start to look like they are encouraging a naive faith in a kindergarten fairy story about everyone doing well and living happily ever after. Are not politics instead fundamentally about conflict and do authentic politics not require an unmasking of opposed interests? This was where the world was in the 1930s, when "realist" interpretations of international relations held sway and when the ideology that was said to underpin liberal internationalism was repeatedly denounced by experts and politicians alike. A liberal view of the world and of the benefits of integration and openness collapsed in the Great Depression. It seems clear today that systemic financial crises like the worldwide catastrophe of the 1930s cause paradigms to shift in ways that threaten to unravel globalization.

Traumatic financial crises usually also involve a new geography of power. One of the most pervasive and persuasive interpretations of the interwar Great Depression was that offered by Charles Kindleberger, who presented the political paralysis as a concomitant of a shift in power from Britain to the United States, from the *pax Britannica* of the late nineteenth century to the *pax Americana* of the late twentieth century.[2] This interpretation influenced many contemporary responses to the events of 2007–2008: a deep financial crisis that emanated in the United States, and which seemed the result of specifically American ways of doing business, must surely be the twenty-first-century equivalent of the British malaise. It is consequently easy to imagine that it marks the beginning of a new and fundamental power shift. Indeed, the German finance minister at an early stage of the development spoke of the 2008 crisis as marking "the end of the American era of global finance."[3]

The challenge to globalization also means that the old debate about the relationship between global integration and state power has come alive again. In particular, many critics of globalization worried that it was eroding the power of the nation-state, and that democratically elected governments were increasingly helpless in the face of the big power of internationally mobile capital, and of large-scale flows of ideas, goods and services, and people. Attempts to control any of these—even the most visible and disturbing of the movements, the migration of people—looked doomed to failure and seemed to herald the end of the nation-state. Politics became rather passive.

Now, with the reversal of financial globalization, we expect the state to protect us from hostile extraneous forces, and the state has become active, even hyperactive, in carrying out this charge. At the same time, the rapid reversal of financial flows has had profoundly destabilizing consequences for the political systems that try to produce a policy response. It has challenged relations of power at a domestic level. And although most people expect that large-scale public-sector action is needed to address the most recent financial meltdown, few realize how the effectiveness of such a policy response is complicated by the international interconnections and interactions that characterize today's economic and political environments. And few realize that only a handful of states are really capable of an effective response.

During the early stages of the 2007–2008 crisis, private-sector solutions to curtail contagion were tried, but they failed in a breathtakingly short time (see Chapter 3). In a financial system that suffers a radical loss of confidence, only institutions with more or less infinite resources can stem the tide. Such institutions can conceivably be self-help organizations, such as pools of powerful banks: that was the case in 1907. But in a climate of profound uncertainty, self-help is not enough. Governments or central banks are needed, because only they are both big and quick enough to address the problem.

The call for a stronger state has become a global phenomenon. The new study by the U.S. National Intelligence Council on what the world will look like in 2025 sketches a future in which "state capitalism" of the kind practiced in China and particularly Russia will be a powerful force to be reckoned with.[4] Key policy decisions, especially in sensitive areas such as energy policy, would be made by state-owned enterprises. Russia's president Medvedev, in a response to American anticrisis measures, concluded triumphantly that "the move from self-regulating capitalism to financial socialism is only one step."[5]

But what kind of government can best tackle the job of putting together the pieces after a financial collapse? Not just any government will do. In the heyday of modern globalization in the 1990s, it looked as if small open states would be the winners of globalization: New Zealand, Chile, Ireland, the Baltic republics, Slovakia, or Slovenia. But already as the next century began, a new vision emerged in which the main beneficiaries would be very large emerging markets with powerful states, the group that Goldman Sachs dubbed the BRICs (Brazil, Russia, India, and China). An alternative way of thinking about them may be as the Big Really Imperial Countries, though this grouping is in reality not as homogenous as the popular BRIC label implies.

In a world in which powerful states have an advantage, even medium-sized states—such as Japan or the larger European states—are not big enough to act effectively on their own. The helplessness is already visible in current debates over European energy policy. Britain, France, or Germany (let alone the much smaller central European countries) cannot tackle issues such as the politics of pipelines crossing Russian territory without a collective negotiating stance. The absence of an effective Europe-wide solution was even more apparent in responses to the 2008 financial crisis. Although banks were active across national frontiers in a single capital and money market, regulation and supervision remained national. Bank support operations, because they were so expensive, were also national affairs. The consequence of this national focus was heightened uncertainty when there was a need to unravel complex cross-national institutions, such as the Belgian-Dutch bank Fortis. The concentration on national solutions also meant in addition that governments were tempted to protect their own institutions the most, so that the national governments engaged in a costly and inefficient regulatory race.

The financial crisis poses a radical alternative: will there be a return to the strong regulatory powers of the nation-state, which evolved in its current form as a response to, and a protection against, the nineteenth-century version of globalization? Or does the logic of dealing with the financial crisis require a regulatory response at a much higher level, and a move to a new style of global government? Either of these steps would be revolutionary for the current world order.

Mid-sized European governments can possibly rescue mid-sized European institutions, but there are probably only two governments rich and influential enough to help the major financial conglomerates at the heart of the world's financial system: the United States and China.

In the similar circumstances of the 1931 financial meltdown, there were also only a limited number of governments that could be effective. The old economic superpower, Britain, was too exhausted and strained to help anyone else. The world's reserves were massively accumulated in the United States.

Thus the only plausible case for a way out of the worldwide Great Depression in 1931 lay, as Kindleberger emphasized, with some step from the United States. At the time, there were all kinds of convincing reasons why Americans should not want to take on the burden of a worldwide rescue: sending more money to Europe might be seen as pouring money down a drain; after all, had not the Europeans fought a world war that had been the fount and origin of the financial mess? Such support would have made a great deal of sense from a long-term economic perspective, but politically, given that it had no short-term payoff, it was a nonstarter.

ONE ALTERNATIVE TO GLOBAL GOVERNANCE: THE UNITED STATES

For more than sixty years, economists and politicians have worried about the central position of the United States and its currency in the international economy. The pessimists started to articulate their doubts before the American party had even begun, with the veteran worrier Melchior Palyi discussing a dollar crisis in 1950 that could "become dangerous if the administration . . . attempts to carry on its huge domestic spending and the foreign aid outlay."[6]

The U.S. dollar had a central role in the 1944 Bretton Woods agreements; the Americans insisted that—in contrast to the early drafts, which envisaged a new, synthetic international reserve currency—other currencies were to have a par value fixed in either gold or U.S. dollars. Other countries, exhausted and devastated by the Second World War, immediately and legitimately began worrying that the United States would impose its monetary preferences on them. In the initial postwar period, there was widespread concern that the dollar would be a permanently scarce currency, and that this would produce a world deflation, similar to that which had followed from the interwar gold standard. By the second half of the 1960s, exactly the opposite argument was made: namely that the United States was forcing inflation on the rest of the world.[7] The international monetary system, according to this account, was a mechanism for transferring the U.S. budget deficits that resulted from the Vietnam War and President Johnson's Great Society program into dollar claims held as international reserves. In consequence, the United States could import goods and services (including those required by its military presence overseas), without really having to pay a price for them, at least for the moment. According to the Belgian economist Robert Triffin, the situation posed two contrasting dangers: that the buildup of dollar claims would go on until the point where investors panicked because they would realize that the claims were unredeemable; and that the U.S. monetary authorities would not expand their money provision sufficiently to meet the world's demand for dollar liquidity.[8]

A frequent criticism, expressed particularly by French policymakers during the late days of the Bretton Woods regime, was that the world was using a "defective clock" as its standard, and would be much better off using a more reliable or constant measure of value, such as gold. In the late 1960s, gold did indeed look like a superior store and measure of value than paper currencies, for which political pressure seemed to lead to endemic high, and increasing, inflation. Since the 1980s, however, monetary policy has been better understood by central banks, and there has been a more general awareness of the benefits of shielding central banks from political pressures to misbehave. The new policy consensus reduced world inflation levels, and paper seemed more stable than gold or silver, now largely demonetized, whose prices over the same period moved quite sharply.

After the fixed-exchange-rate regime collapsed in 1971–1973, no legal obligation existed to define the value of currencies in terms of dollars. But the dollar remained the key currency, to the extent that some economists by the beginning of the new millennium were referring to the international financial system as a "Bretton Woods Mark Two" regime.[9] Many rapidly growing emerging markets were de facto targeting a particular exchange rate against the U.S. dollar. The result was a series of remarkable similarities to the world of fixed exchange rates as they had existed in the 1960s, including the hegemonic role of the U.S.

dollar, with the dollar as the major reserve currency; the deliberate use of the exchange-rate regime by rapidly growing economies (Germany and Japan in the 1960s, the Asian economies after the 1990s) to secure employment growth via export promotion; the widespread demand for dollars, which has allowed the financing of U.S. current account deficits for very long periods of time, though perhaps not indefinitely; and finally, the strategic dominance of the United States. As in previous eras, the new order also generated expectations of a coming financial crisis by those who were suspicious of or hostile to American strategic dominance.

Every decade since 1971 has produced new and slightly differently formulated worries about the American position and its allegedly inherent unsustainability. At first, the dollar exchange rate remained (largely for trade reasons) a key issue of concern. French president Valéry Giscard d'Estaing, at the first world economic summit at Rambouillet in 1975, denounced flexible exchange rates as a "decadent" idea that fostered the abuse of monetary standards.[10] In the late 1970s, the persistence of high inflation in the United States and weakness in the dollar motivated French and German leaders to move forward with monetary integration at the European level. In the mid-1980s, a high valuation of the dollar (following from a combination of an anti-inflationary monetary policy and a highly expansive fiscal policy) made other countries worried that the U.S. political system would respond to the erosion of jobs in manufacturing with trade protection. This concern was used as a lever by the United States to pry open (or "liberalize") other economies, notably in Japan but also in Western Europe. In 1988 Robert Triffin renewed his critique of the "fantastic U.S. deficits and capital imports," which he described as "unsustainable as well as unacceptable," and revived the idea of a substitution account denominated in an artificial or synthetic currency. In the early 1990s, Robert Z. Lawrence announced that deteriorating competitiveness resulting from falling labor-productivity rates meant the "end of the American dream."[11] By 2009, it was China that was reviving the idea of managing international reserves with a composite currency as well as replicating the French strategy of the 1960s in holding an increasing share of its foreign exchange in gold rather than dollars.

The world in reality still remained a dollar-based system, in part because the United States was still the world's largest single market. The overwhelming majority of commodity prices were still denominated in dollars, which led to an obvious rationale for many countries to continue to hold reserves in dollars. In fact, the dollar share of international reserves, which had fallen from 73 percent in 1978 to below 50 percent by the end of the 1980s, surged again to a peak of 71 percent in 1999–2001, before a modest fall to 66.5 percent in 2005 and 63.8 percent by the third quarter of 2007.[12] A large part of the changes, however, represents simply valuation effects following from the rise of the dollar in the 1990s, and its subsequent fall, rather than decisions to shift portfolios, even in 2007, when the dollar-exchange rate fell rapidly. The implications of such an analysis are comforting to those concerned with the longer-term position of the dollar.

The question of the current account is inevitably political. The current account, or the difference between goods and services imported and exported, which is financed through flows of surplus savings, only matters because of the existence of separate currencies controlled by distinct political entities. There may thus be massive differences in savings and investment levels between New Jersey and California, corresponding to a flow of funds or a current account "imbalance," but no one really notices or minds, because these states are in a single currency area. If there were one world currency, as some writers such as Robert Mundell and in a more nuanced form Richard Cooper have advocated, then there would also be no need to debate the current account position of the United States, even though the real effects of a Chinese "undervaluation" would still be noticeable as a surge in job creation but reduced wealth levels (with the opposite effect in the United States). Indeed, precisely this effect can be seen in contemporary Europe, where Germany has an "undervalued" currency and has created jobs while suffering low income growth. The currency union takes away the political dynamite from the process (unless enough people notice what is happening). But with a separate currency, the surplus or deficit is political, and pressure to change the exchange-rate policy can thus emerge. In this sense, the current account does matter.

There are two ways of approaching the story of the current account. The first is as the outcome of levels of savings and investment, in which a surplus of savings would produce a current account surplus and cause the export of the difference between savings and investment, and a savings deficit would need to be financed by inflows from abroad. The second considers the current account as combined investment income minus net payments for goods and services.

The current account position of the United States reflects a long-term shift. In 1946, the current account surplus was 3.9 percent of GDP, with a merchandise trade balance of $6.7 billion and a (non-military) services balance of $1.0 billion. The United States had built up a substantial creditor position in the world economy, which became even bigger over the next thirty years as American corporations invested all over the world and transformed the local economies of Western Europe and Japan. Net investment income in 1946 amounted to $560 million. By 1971, when the international monetary system built around the fixed-exchange-rate (Bretton Woods) regime collapsed, the current account had shrunk to a small deficit, equivalent to 0.1 percent of GDP, and there was a negative merchandise balance (−$2.3 billion), a small surplus on services, and very substantial earnings from the investment assets built up overseas over the previous twenty years ($7.3 billion). In 1985, when tight monetary policies combined with a big fiscal deficit sent the dollar to a spiky peak, there was a large current account deficit of $118.2 billion, or 2.8 percent of GDP, and a surge in earnings

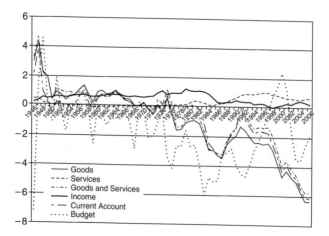

U.S. budget and current account position, with surpluses and deficits shown as a percentage of GDP, 1946–2006.

Source: Council of Economic Advisers, Economic Report of the President, 2008.

from investment of $25.7 billion. At this point, the United States became a net debtor, and a major recipient of foreign inflows, but the earnings on investment remained very high through the 1990s, as the U.S. debtor position became ever more extreme.

The large-scale capital movements that supported the U.S. dollar in the 1990s and 2000s were only in part the consequence of the reserve policies of the

Chinese and other Asian central banks. The flows present a puzzle. Usually, most economists assumed, capital should flow from rich to poor countries, where there is a greater potential for technological catch-up. While such flows characterized much of the 1970s, they did not take place (on a net basis) when the real era of modern globalization began, in the 1980s. As mentioned earlier, from the mid-1980s, the United States became a net debtor (as it had been before the First World War), and by the millennium, the United States accounted for some three-quarters of the world's net capital imports (the other big borrowers were the United Kingdom and Australia).

The large and counterintuitive inflow of capital to the United States was at first explained by many analysts as an idiosyncratic response to the Latin American debt crisis of the early 1980s, which appeared to reverse the direction of capital flows. Subsequently other essentially short-term reasons have been given, including at times the attractions of the U.S. stock market and the U.S. real estate boom.

A phenomenon that has been in existence for more than twenty years, however, seems to call for a structural explanation rather than the concatenation of a series of more or less chance influences. The long-term propensity of the late-twentieth-century United

States to import capital could be explained either through supply factors (changes in the global supply of savings, as a result of more widespread development outside the established industrial countries), or demand factors (why the United States is an attractive investment).

In the final period of the credit boom at the start of the twenty-first century, the United States attracted a large amount of official inflows, much of which went into the mortgage bonds of the government-sponsored agencies Fannie Mae and Freddie Mac. By 2008, it was estimated that foreign holders accounted for $1.3 trillion of agency bond holdings. The largest amount was held by China, with substantial amounts also in Russian hands.[13]

Money flowed to the United States not for higher returns but because the United States seemed a secure investment option. Oddly enough, the yield on U.S. assets for foreigners, that is, the price paid by the United States for its borrowing, is substantially lower than the yield for Americans on their foreign holdings. (This disparity explains why the balance on investment income continues to be so surprisingly resilient and large.) The economists Pierre-Olivier Gourinchas and Hélène Rey have calculated that for the whole period 1960 to 2001, the annualized rate of return on U.S. liabilities (3.61 percent) was more than two percentage points below the annualized real rate of return on U.S. assets (5.72 percent), and that for the post-1973 period the difference is significantly larger (the respective figures are 3.50 and 6.82 percent).[14] The yield difference reflects not miscalculation or stupidity on the part of foreign investors, but a decision to buy security in return for lower yields. The primary attraction of the United States as a destination for capital movement is the unique depth of its markets (which generates financial security) and its steady political and security positions. Few other countries share the reputation of the United States as a stable and secure haven in which property rights are powerfully protected. As a consequence, inflows to the United States may increase after global security shocks (as they did after the terrorist attacks of September 11, 2001, and again after the financial debacle of September 14, 2008). The result is counterintuitive, and irritating to many non-Americans: why does the collapse of a big American institution make the United States a more secure place?

Before 2007, some economists argued that business-cycle volatility in the United States had fallen substantially since the early 1980s (the so-called great moderation) relative to volatility in other major economies. This interpretation may even be borne out in the extreme circumstances of the current crisis, where though the United States has experienced an enormous shock, it looks benign compared to the massive collapses in production in some of the world's biggest exporters (Germany and Japan), and in many emerging markets in central Europe, South Asia, and East Asia. [15]

But reduced volatility lowers the incentives to accumulate precautionary savings, and the dramatic fall in the U.S. savings rate, above all in the level of personal savings, meant that the United States has needed to attract an inflow of surplus savings from elsewhere. Personal saving fell from 10.1 percent of income in the last quarter of 1970, to 6.9 percent in 1990, and then even more precipitously to 1.9 percent in 2000 and 0.8 percent in 2005.[16] The collapse of American savings was so dramatic that it led many commentators to see it as the major driver of the "global imbalances" that required massive international financial intermediation.

It is worth thinking further about what allowed countries like the United States and the United Kingdom to continue to attract money with low rates of return over extended (but not infinite) periods of time. What motivation drove the inflows? Two types of capital market centers coexisted in the modern era of globalization. Some small dynamic intermediaries attracted large inflows, but also recycled or reexported those funds and even had large current account surpluses: for 2005, Hong Kong had a surplus of 11.4 percent of GDP; Singapore, 28.5 percent; Luxembourg, 9.7 percent; and Switzerland, 13.8 percent. The larger intermediaries before the crisis, by contrast, were major capital importers: the United States, with a current account deficit of 6.4 percent of GDP; Australia with a 6.0 percent deficit; and the United Kingdom with a more modest 2.2 percent deficit. These larger countries feature a generally affluent lifestyle and clusters of workers with specific skills in high-value-added sectors, as well as renowned institutions of higher education that attracted substantial numbers of skilled immigrants. Such immigration might have substantially raised their potential and probable growth rates. These large countries relied on their size as well as their image as homes to the Good Life to help make them not only appealing assets, but also secure in both a political and economic sense.

The role of migration in this story has been relatively neglected in the literature that discusses security and stability, as well as in that which addresses the sustainability of current account imbalances. Immigration often is associated with optimism on the part of the migrants, and one of the consequences of a more generalized optimism is a belief in higher future returns. Such attitudes will tend to produce lower rates of savings. By contrast, emigrant societies (especially those with the low birth rates characteristic of much of Europe and Japan) are worried about falling future returns, and consequently the motives for precautionary saving are much stronger.

The U.S.-style Good Life is not simply a commitment to high levels of consumption. Contrary to popular belief, particularly outside the United States, the consumption story that drives the growing current account imbalance is not fundamentally the result of an addiction to outrageous forms of conspicuous consumption such as SUVs.[17] (Though there are some odd statistics that seem to support parts of this thesis: for example, Americans spent more on jewelry in the early twenty-first century than on shoes.[18]) But expenditure on food and clothing as a proportion of income has fallen dramatically over recent decades, and expenditure on housing remains more or less constant. Instead the big growth in spending has been in the areas of education and health. Many academic economists (who have an obvious interest as educators) would like to reclassify these as forms of investment in human capital, and it is probably true that the continued innovative capacity of the United States depends on quality education. Such a link between higher education (investment in human capital) and economic growth is the subject of much research.[19] Good education promotes inflows of highly skilled labor, which indeed picked up notably in the last decades of the twentieth century. Thus a 2005 study by the U.S. Committee on Science, Engineering, and Public Policy showed that the proportion of doctorates granted to non-U.S. students in science and engineering rose from 23 percent in 1966 to 39 percent in 2000. The United States benefits greatly by attracting highly educated people from other parts of the world, and the export of people trained in American universities is a vital part of Joseph Nye's idea of "soft power."[20] Highly educated continental Europeans have become extremely mobile and leave their countries, often for Anglo-Saxon destinations. In consequence, London has become the fourth largest French city, with an estimated 400,000 French citizens in London and the South-East.[21] Australia has become a similar magnet for highly dynamic and educated Asians. But the

United States remains the most popular destination for the world's educated mobile elite.

Another element of the overconsumption theory arises from the link between fiscal issues and the current account. Some part of the story can be explained by government dis-saving, rather than by household choices. This link is more obviously and directly political. Government spending on the military is a form of consumption, and in the Vietnam era, during the Reagan defense buildup, and again in the post-2001 world, military expenditures became a controversial issue in international discussions of monetary and financial stability. In all these cases, the defense buildup went hand in hand with domestically oriented fiscal expansion (examples include when President Johnson created the Great Society, and Presidents Reagan and George W. Bush cut taxes). It is as if the United States could not gather the domestic support for defense or war without buying social contentment at home through an expansive fiscal policy. Federal spending is thus part of a large package that underpins in the broadest sense the security of the United States. Capital markets respond in turn to the heightened sense of security. The historical precedents mean that the world is well prepared to tolerate even the enormous fiscal stimuli of the February 2009 plan of President Obama, or the 8.8 percent budget deficit projected for 2009.

The conceptualization of the U.S. position as a banker or international financial intermediary was made already in the 1960s, when Kindleberger and others presented a view on why the apparently deteriorating U.S. external payments position was more sustainable than it seemed.[22] Viewed in this perspective, the United States was in the position of a bank, taking short-term deposits from those who wanted security, and earning a return by lending these deposits out long-term and to riskier borrowers. We tend to trust bigger banks more, because we think that they are better able to absorb shocks. Such a position, however, contains two sets of risks: first, that the lenders (depositors) might come to think of the United States as in some way less secure; and second, that they might be worried about the bank's lending policy and the solvency of its borrowers. The modern equivalent to Kindleberger's 1960s "United States as a bank" analogy would be that the United States is the equivalent of a global hedge fund, taking risks elsewhere on substantial leverage in the belief that the world as a whole is becoming more secure and hence that risk premiums will fall over the long term. The links among global enrichment, peace, and American superior strategic capability were made in a very striking way in a September 2002 National Security document.[23] But doubts about the place of the United States in the world since 2003 have helped to make it look financially less stable and secure.

The ability of the United States to take bets on the American economy and the American financial franchise depends on the assessment of others that the country is indeed stable, and that worldwide pacification is a strategy that is paying off. Thus in the first place the ability of the United States to finance its deficits depends on the continued perception that it is a high-growth, high-productivity economy and that it is politically and militarily secure. That confidence could clearly be shaken by terrorist attacks on U.S. territory, particularly were they to employ atomic, biological, or chemical weapons. It is also possible to imagine how financial attacks might be mobilized by rivals in the great game of international power politics. There are historical examples in which European countries, for instance, have used speculative financial attacks against their competitors in order to obtain a security advantage. France in the 1911 Morocco crisis tried in this fashion to instrumentalize a run on the German market, while in the mid-1930s German agents encouraged speculation against the French franc. In both cases, the hope was that a financial crisis would not only shake the rival, but also and most immediately force fiscal action, which would involve cutting back defense expenditures.

Conversely, the security of the United States depends on the continued inflow of capital; any sudden adjustment to the current situation would be unbearably painful and intolerable politically. This is why the sustainability discussion is so central to estimates of the future path of the international order. If capital were withdrawn or even just slowed, a vicious cycle would commence, in which the political stake of other countries in American stability would be reduced, and even more rapid outflows would occur.

The scenario is not as far-fetched as it may seem. As the financial crisis worsened in early 2009, the Chinese leadership began to demand guarantees that its holding of U.S. government debt would not be devalued or expropriated—with the implied threat that without such a guarantee, U.S. debt would be a less attractive investment to the Chinese in the future. At the same time, it has increased its gold holdings. It is this nightmare scenario of declining investment in U.S. debt that lies at the heart of the influentially gloomy commentaries and websites of Nouriel

Roubini, Kenneth Rogoff, and Brad DeLong. So it is worth looking back at previous nightmare scenarios.

In the post–Bretton Woods world, there have been several moments when the United States no longer appeared to be so secure, and when a political as well as an economic logic drove the movement of capital out of the country. At these moments of shock, capital outflows seemed to be related to the questioning of the solidity of U.S. institutions. The first of such crisis moments occurred in the early 1970s, when the par value system broke down just as the United States was trying to extricate itself from a failed war in Vietnam. In the late 1970s, too, a (second) oil price shock seemed to raise new questions about the stability of the United States. Again there were major outflows, as well as a rapid depreciation of the dollar.

Developments since 2001 bear some analogies to these earlier moments of doubt about the permanence of U.S. stability. As in previous episodes there are apparently unrelated sources of doubt: the failure of U.S. grand strategy throughout the world, but also worries about the response of U.S. lawmakers to the corporate scandals at the turn of the millennium (which produced a pendulum shift toward much heavier and more complex corporate regulation, in particular the Sarbanes-Oxley Act's provisions on enhanced accounting standards) and the likely responses to the post-2007 financial crisis, which will be far more radical and extensive.

Since the early 1960s, alarmists have felt that the position of the United States in the international monetary system was unsustainable. Charles de Gaulle's criticism of the United States seems a peculiarly timeless example of the European view that could have been made at any point over the past forty years: "The United States is not capable of balancing its budget. It allows itself to have enormous debts. Since the dollar is the reference currency everywhere, it can cause others to suffer the effects of its poor management. This is not acceptable. This cannot last."[24] Such critiques of the American role were taken up again in the mid-1980s, and once more after the turn of the millennium. They usually come from people who have doubts about the value of the Good Life as practiced in its modern epicenters. For them, the Good Life is associated with the projection of power, the instigation of inequality, and the canonization of consumption and cupidity.

There is an obvious contrast of U.S. deficits with the long-sustained British experience of *pax Britannica*. The resilience of the British empire owed a great deal to its long-term current account surplus position from the mid-nineteenth century to the First World War, but it was then weakened by the massive fiscal expenditure that followed from military conflict. The "cannot last" issue raises the link between the capacity to borrow and the dependence of this capacity on continued economic dynamism. In the late nineteenth-century era of open capital markets, inflows to high-growth countries (such as the United States or Australia) were sustained over very long periods, above all because (then as now) capital inflows were accompanied by migration flows in which labor moved over large distances and across national frontiers into higher productivity occupations. The result generated income gains both in the senders and the receivers of the migrations. The question about sustainability then turns into one about the probability of continuing to achieve growth rates that are higher than those of the rest of the industrialized world. How long will the United States be able to occupy such a position?

Growth rates are threatened by long-term fiscal problems arising from both military commitments and the burdens of ensuring social security for an aging population: in this the United States shares (in a less extreme form) a problem that is also emerging in the aging industrial societies of Europe and Japan.[25] The deterioration of the fiscal position in the beginning of the millennium was a transnational phenomenon: the average general government fiscal balance for all the advanced industrial economies in 2000 was exactly in balance, while in 2004 the figure had slid to a deficit of 3.9 percent. There then was a general improvement, followed by the emergence of much larger deficits in most of the major industrial countries in 2009 in response to the financial and economic crisis.

Fiscal problems pose a long-term threat to the capacity of not only the United States but also other large industrial countries to sustain growth and hence capital inflows. The liquidity produced by the new large international transfers of capital have produced a trap in which it is easy for governments (but not necessarily corporations) of the large advanced countries to borrow very cheaply. In the context of the worsening financial crisis and growing fiscal deficits, this part of the exorbitant privilege of being big and rich began to be questioned. In particular, by early 2009, China was posing increasingly worried questions about the sustainability of the large U.S. debt.

Some long-term prognoses are possible. It is probable that the availability of funding for the big governments of the major industrial countries will become more constrained in the future. Emerging markets presently characterized by unusually high rates of saving will "graduate" and become more like advanced industrial countries, in other words, less inclined to produce big surpluses of capital for export. It is safe to assume that the graduation would be accompanied first by a rise in consumption by individuals, as the precautionary motive for saving in conditions of insecurity gradually diminishes. But it is also likely that such governments will be tempted to behave more like the advanced countries and increase their spending, on infrastructure in order to maintain the economic miracle, as well as on social expenditures, since these countries too face the issue of aging populations. Most likely, however, is an increase in expenditure on technology items that have a military potential, and that can thus help increase their power in the international order.

A very long-term comparative perspective on past episodes of imperial rule also suggests some analogies. The ease with which the United States and other big countries can finance their deficits bears a resemblance to the most famous case of long, drawn-out imperial decline, that of Habsburg Spain.[26] The equivalent to the inflows of funds to all the advanced countries in the last decades of the twentieth century was the story of New World silver, which initially appeared as a source of immense strategic power. It let Spain have something (mostly the services of troops) apparently for nothing; just as in other cases there can appear to be a "free lunch" for the hegemon. The inflow of silver did not immediately lead to Spanish decline, but it did eventually produce a hollowing out of the Spanish economy and in the end also a loss of strategic preeminence. Such analogies suggest not an immediate collapse as a result of the twenty-first-century global imbalances, but the basis for a longer-term shift in power and influence. In the course of that shift, the security advantages that constitute currently the major advantage of the United States (and the real source of the unique or exorbitant privilege of the dollar) are likely to fade.

Another way of making this point is to say that maintaining the dollar as a stable store of value will become a more costly option when foreigners as well as Americans see American stability in less rosy terms than they did at the end of the twentieth century and the beginning of the new millennium.

Of course, the world has been in that situation before. States, especially hegemonic states, face a constant danger of overspending their capital and hence of ruin in the manner described by Adam Smith: "The progress of the enormous debts which at present oppress, and will in the long-run probably ruin, all the great nations of Europe, has been pretty uniform. . . . When national debts have once been accumulated to a certain degree, there is scarce, I believe, a single instance of their having been fairly and completely paid. The liberation of the public revenue, if it has ever been brought about at all, has always been brought about by a bankruptcy; sometimes by an avowed one, but always by a real one, though frequently by a pretended payment."[27]

The U.S. dollar will be the major international currency as long as the United States remains the world's largest concentration of political and military might as well as of economic potential.[28] Economic and political power tend to go hand in hand in a world that is insecure and at the same time places a high value on security and growth. Such concentrations of power can be self-sustaining when they attract not only the capital resources, but also the human resources (primarily through skilled immigration) that allow exceptional productivity growth to continue. When and if they close themselves off to sources of innovation—as Golden Age Spain did—the process of relative decline becomes much faster.

Since the isolationist impulse is a major strand in the American political tradition, it is impossible to close off this possibility; in fact, its likelihood increases as the economic and financial situation deteriorates.

ANOTHER ALTERNATIVE TO GLOBAL GOVERNANCE: THE EUROPEAN UNION

The replacement of the dollar as a reserve currency has been widely predicted. Scholars such as Barry Eichengreen and Marcello de Cecco, for instance, see the rise of the euro as an alternative store of value.[29] China is now pushing for a synthetic reserve currency, in the form of the IMF's Special Drawing Rights (SDRs), in which the euro has a great weighting. Indeed, for Eichengreen, the euro is the major reason why the "Bretton Woods Two" interpretation by Michael Dooley, David Folkerts-Landau, and Peter Garber is implausible, and why the analogy with the 1960s should not be convincing: "The difference today is the euro. The large, liquid market in euro-denominated government securities provides an attractive alternative to holding United States treasury bonds for the central banks of emerging markets."[30]

But there are as many uncertainties about the future of the euro as about the dollar. In fact, the European Union is suffering from a number of problems that have been widely discussed for many years, but just never seemed to be that urgent. Suddenly, in the face of the economic crisis, these issues have become major sources of political vulnerability and instability.

Granted, there is a common monetary policy in the Eurozone countries, and an integrated capital market with financial institutions that are active across national frontiers. But banks are regulated and supervised nationally. The regulators need to be national because in the event of a large bank failure, any bank rescue becomes a fiscal issue. Since the cost is carried by the taxpayer in individual states, and not by the European Union as a whole, such national supervision makes sense politically. But the fiscally constrained national setting makes little sense in the face of the economic logic of European integration.

The explosion of the U.S. financial crisis into an emerging-market crisis added a new dimension to the threat of banking instability in Europe. The exposure of banks to currency risk both in central European member states of the EU (notably in Poland, Hungary, the Czech Republic, and Latvia), as well as in nonmember states such as Ukraine, is particularly high for some of the smaller members of the EU, especially Austria. Austrian banks have an exposure to their eastern neighbors that is estimated at €230 billion, or 70 percent of Austrian GDP.

The second well-known problem lies in the macroeconomic difficulties of the euro area. Since the introduction of a single currency and the locking of European exchange rates in 1999, wages and productivity have taken a different course in Mediterranean Europe, Spain, Portugal, Greece, and Italy, than in the north, especially in Germany. In the past, divergences in measures of competitiveness were solved by altering the exchange rate. The euro made this impossible. Countries like Italy, with a different historical product range and with exports in leather, textiles, and clothing and in such consumer goods as white products (refrigerators, washing machines), were more vulnerable to competition from fast-growing emerging-market economies than was Germany, which had historically focused on engineering goods. But the competitive divergence exaggerated a tendency that arose because of product structure.

A third obvious problem is the disciplining effect of fiscal rules. Fiscal control has been the subject of long-standing debate since the Maastricht treaties on political and monetary union and the apparently inflexible restrictions they imposed on government debts and deficits. The European Union's budget is tiny relative to those of the member states, and the vast part of European government expenditure occurs on a national level. But differing debt levels mean that the various national governments have very different amounts of fiscal wiggle room. Italian, Greek, or Portuguese public debt is so high that any attempt to use fiscal spending to help combat the economic crisis is doomed to fail. Ireland, which previously had only modest deficit and debt levels, also suddenly and unexpectedly has the same kind of constraint, because of the scope and cost of its banking crisis and the consequent need to move private debt from the banking sector into the hands of the government. France and Germany, by contrast, have an inherently strong fiscal position. Given this radical inequality in policy choices, the European Union as a whole is powerless, and only its strongest member countries can really do anything against the sharply worsening recession.

Moreover, the idea of Keynesian demand stimulus as a response to economic downturn was an intellectual product of the depression era of the 1930s. It emerged in the context of self-contained national economies. Keynesians used the warm water of fiscal stimulus to fill up a national bathtub. When the national bathtub has holes, and other people benefit from the warmth, the exercise loses its attraction. In addition, Keynesianism only ever worked for the larger states. The smaller states could not do Keynesianism in a hand basin without constraining and impoverishing themselves.

There might have been ways to fix both the banking and the fiscal problem for European politics. Control of banking is the simplest. The European Central Bank clearly has the technical and analytic capacity to take on a general supervision of European banks, using the member central banks as conduits of information. Its officials recently have pleaded for such an extension of their mission.[31] But in a situation where massive bank bailouts and rescues are likely to be needed, the question is raised of how the costs of any fiscal response are to be shared among the different national governments. One plausible and attractive suggestion is to support bank reconstruction by issuing generally guaranteed European bonds. Such action might be conceived as a temporary measure, restricted to the financial emergency. But it is opposed by national governments, especially in the larger countries, who fear that a crisis measure

might provide the basis for a permanent shift of responsibility—and of political power.

Both effective bank regulation and fiscal policy
measures to respond to the economic and financial
crisis pose an acute dilemma. They require either a
move to more Europeanization, or a backward move
to reverse the integration of the previous decades.
The most obvious way to Europeanize more is to use
existing mechanisms and institutions, in particular
the European Central Bank or the European Commission. But each has its problems: the European
Central Bank developed largely outside the framework of the European Union, as an extension of the
Basel Committee of Central Bank Governors of the
Member Countries of the European Economic Community, and the European Commission has long
been gridlocked.

But even if a common institution could rise to the
challenge, there would still be political problems to
overcome. Greater Europeanization implies a relative
weakening of the national states, including the large
states, Germany and France, which have become once
more the key players in the European process. In consequence, they will resist, and try to stay in their own
national Keynesian bathtubs—regulating only their
own banks because in that way alone they can ensure

that they will direct bank credit to their taxpayers and voters, in other words, to their political constituencies.

There is a historical precedent for the proclivity of Paris and Berlin to think nationally. Indeed a recent and convincing account by David Marsh depicts the evolution of the euro primarily in terms of a power play between France and Germany, which Germany won.[32] In the current crisis environment, it is clear that from the perspective of Germany or France, there should be no systematic Europeanization. Instead, these larger states are now promoting informal groupings that look for worldwide solutions. The result has been a frenetic turbo-charged activism, an acceleration of the timetable of meetings of different sorts of groups, some involving members of the Eurozone, others involving non-Eurozone members such as the United Kingdom. The institutional coherence of the European project has dissipated rather than been strengthened in Europe's response to the financial crisis.

In the second half of the twentieth century, Europe had the chance to build a much more benevolent form of regionalism. But today it is stymied by having lost the chance to build stronger institutions when times were better and tempers less strained. As a consequence, the suspicions about regionalism in Europe evoke more and more the ghosts of the 1930s. The most unattractive versions of 1930s regionalism came from Germany and Japan, and represented nothing less than a practical extension of German and Japanese power over smaller and vulnerable neighbors. Germany and Japan did not simply keep their nationalism to themselves. Neighbors were forced into trade and financial dependence on the German Grosswirtschaftsraum ("greater economic area") or the Japanese equivalent, the Greater East Asia Co-Prosperity Sphere. As a result of the horrors of the 1930s, there is still substantial suspicion of concepts like "Greater East Asia."

Overtones of the 1930s are amplified because of an odd coincidence. The chance of the rotating presidency has rather clearly exposed the EU's predicament. The Czech Republic, probably the country with the most vivid historical memory of the bad regionalism of the 1930s, at the beginning of 2009 took over the EU presidency from France, the European country that is today least constrained in its assertion of national interest. Two visions of Europe are now clashing, one concerned with equal treatment of members, and one concerned with the power realities of the large states. This conflict is quickly eroding the political stability of an area that once represented the world's best model for a benign regionalism.

China is the America of this century. The initial stages of the credit crunch in 2007 were managed so apparently painlessly because sovereign wealth funds (SWFs) from the Middle East, but above all from China, were willing to step in and recapitalize the debt of American and European institutions. If this process had continued, the events of 2008 would have looked rather more like 1929, in other words, problems with U.S. real estate, a severe stock market decline, but no meltdown of financial institutions.

Between November 2007 and March 2008, the SWFs provided $41 billion of the $105 billion injected into major financial institutions. The Abu Dhabi Investment Authority took a stake in Citigroup, the Singapore Investment Corporation in the Swiss bank UBS, the China Investment Corporation in Morgan Stanley. The Singapore fund Temasek explained its decision in terms of the "underlying strength of Merrill Lynch's franchise."[33] But in March 2008, the availability of funds to prop up the world's financial system shriveled up. The pivotal moment in today's events came when the Chinese SWF China Investment Corporation (CIC) was unwilling to go further in its exploration of buying Lehman Brothers. The CIC's turning back, like the Creditanstalt crisis of 1931 (described in Chapter 2) will be held up in the future as a moment when history could have turned in a different direction.

The emerging markets hold out to the world the hope that they are the new providers of capital in the global system. Some commentators, including the influential *Financial Times* commentator Martin Wolf, see this credit provision as the driving force behind the global bubble of the early twenty-first century that then inevitably burst. According to Wolf's interpretation, China followed an "inordinately mercantilist currency policy."[34] This policy caused the emergence of the global imbalances that then grew due to the attractions of the U.S. market, as described earlier. In order to push out exports, and to keep a vast and potentially restive workforce occupied, China prevented the exchange rate from appreciating and making Chinese exports more expensive.[35] The result was a vast trade surplus: the monument to modern mercantilism. The byproduct, mostly unintended, was the piling up of dollar reserves, which China placed mostly in U.S. government securities, though quasi-state institutions such as Fannie Mae and Freddie Mac were also beneficiaries. These assets were earning a very poor return, and indeed the rapid depreciation of the dollar meant that China's reward for its creditor status was actually negative. (The United States can clearly print as many dollars as it wants, and in this way may gradually effectively expropriate the holders of assets denominated in its currency.) China, or rather its citizens, thus has had to pay a high price for its mercantilism. This interpretation represents an international version of Governor Sarah Palin's response in the vice presidential television debate of 2008: "Darn right, it was the predatory lenders." The predators were the Chinese, and many Americans wanted to see them punished.

After the financial crisis, the ability to supply new credit will translate into political power. China and other Asian economies are not only currently the major world generators of savings; they are also likely to continue to have high savings rates in the medium (ten- to twenty-year) term. In the 1990s and 2000s, rapidly growing but politically unstable and insecure countries experienced dramatic rises in their savings rates, as citizens felt unsure about their futures and unable to rely on state support mechanisms. China's medical provision, for example, became increasingly expensive, and access to medical care harder. In the absence of the safety net of national pensions, national health, and old-age assistance, citizens need to self-insure. With further growth, financial development, and new functions for the state, savings rates will decline, but such a trend will be a very long-term development.

The paradigmatic case is that of China, where, although in absolute terms consumption rose, rates of consumption fell as incomes rose: by 2005, Chinese households were consuming less than 40 percent of GDP, and Chinese households had moved to very high savings rates (of around 30 percent). With simultaneous high saving by the government and by enterprises, the outcome is a large amount of capital in search of security. The savings surge, and the accompanying positive current account balance, are not just Chinese peculiarities, but can be found in most Asian, South Asian, and Middle Eastern economies. As credit disintermediation sets in, savers are likely to want to place their money in institutions nearer home that they can have more confidence in, rather than in obscure banks on the other side of the world. The move to a simplified and more transparent financial system (see Chapter 4) will speed this transition by strengthening Chinese financial institutions. And as these institutions determine how and where the pooled savings resources of China's population will flow, they will become the important players in the world economy. Indeed, by the beginning of 2009, the largest three banks in the world by market value were Chinese: the Industrial and Commercial Bank of China, the China Construction Bank, and the Bank of China.

Today there are plenty of reasons that the Chinese might be tempted to pull back from their engagement with the world economy. In fact, the external political logic sounds like the American case of 1931. Some of the arguments that are reverberating around Beijing are reasonable: there is a great deal of uncertainty, and the SWFs might lose a lot of money—CIC, for example, would have initially lost some money with Lehman. Other lines of thought are more emotional: might not 2008 be a payback for the American bungling of the 1997–1998 East Asia crisis?

There is still an undoubted dynamism in the Chinese economy. The strength of the domestic market meant that growth continued, albeit at a reduced pace, even in the grim circumstances of 2008 and 2009. In late 2008, China announced one of the largest national stimulus packages of 4 trillion RMB (or $585 billion). Unlike most of the major industrial countries, public debt is quite limited. Even the gigantic spending program will only push it up to about a quarter of GDP, so there is fiscal room for further infrastructure projects.

At the same time, there is a myriad of domestic reasons—financial, social, demographic, and political—that China might be expected to be vulnerable. The Chinese banking system is still quite opaque, and may still have to wrestle with the legacy of problems of the 1990s, in particular politically directed bad loans to big state-owned corporations. China is investing large amounts in education, but it may be difficult to make a creative and innovative society that replicates the dynamism of the United States in the second half of the twentieth century (which was in large part fed by openness, including above all openness to immigration). There is the familiar problem of an aging population and even an anticipated demographic decline after the 2040s as a legacy of the one-child policy and of a major imbalance between a surplus of young males and an artificially reduced female population. An authoritarian though reformist regime may find it harder to respond flexibly to popular demands, and may be prone to try to mobilize a reactive nationalism to fend off challenges to its authority.

The pressure to engage in large-scale fiscal stimulation is also likely to alter the balance of China's economic development. Even before the outbreak of the economic crisis, there were two alternative models of Chinese economic development. The first was the rural-oriented, family- and small-business-based boom of the 1980s, and it laid a solid foundation for China's modern economic miracle. But by the 1990s, some of the private-sector growth was being choked off by a rival vision of economic growth, built around prestige projects and the large state-owned enterprise sector. This rival vision has its critics. While many impressed commentators have described Shanghai as the most modern city in the world, analysts of the Chinese economy have suggested that it is one of the least entrepreneurial cities in China. The scholar Yasheng Huan has described it as "a classic industrial-policy state."[36] The new stimulus package with its heavy emphasis on infrastructure investment is likely to push the balance of Chinese development more decisively in this latter direction.

China thus has plenty of reasons why it might want to close itself off to the forces of globalization, as the United States did in some policy areas during the Great Depression era (especially regarding immigration and trade in the 1920s and in finance during the 1930s). Once again, the experience of the 1930s seems to hold some unattractive precedents. The United States felt uncomfortable with the international institutions of the interwar period in part because they were aligned with the interests of the old hegemonic power, Britain. The League of Nations looked as if it was in practice a tool of British power. Similarly, in the modern context China worries about whether it is adequately represented in international institutions. Its influence in the International Monetary Fund and the World Trade Organization clearly does not correspond to its real position in the world economy, and to the role that China could play in economic stabilization. Reforming international institutions in order to encompass the geopolitical shift is thus a key issue for determining whether the geopolitical alterations will be crisis-ridden, abrupt, and disruptive, or whether a more gradual and peaceful path of adjustment can be achieved.

International institutions are shaped around the leading powers of the day. The international architecture needs to reflect the concerns and interests of the leading powers, if it is to be effective. But in turn, the international architecture is a way of locking those great powers into internationalism, as the postwar institutions did very successfully in the case of the United States.[37]

We are about to see what stake China really has in the survival of the globalized world economy. As in 1931, the political arguments are all about China's not knuckling under to support the current world system. A bestseller published in early 2009, *Unhappy China,* urged the People's Republic to stand up to the West and assert its rights as a superpower. Only the far-sighted will see the attractions of the economic case for a rescue through the continued flow of financial resources—a case based on the argument that China's rise is inextricably linked with an open and prosperous world economy. (Not coincidentally, this was the kind of argument that Cordell Hull tried to push all through the 1930s and 1940s.) The arguments that convince Chinese leaders will, however, be fundamentally political rather than economic. Just before the Asia-Europe Meeting of October 24, 2008, China's president, Hu Jintao, stated that China would behave "with a sense of responsibility." The way to draw China in is to promise the country's leadership a stronger voice in an altered international institutional architecture. Increased representation in quotas and votes at the International Monetary Fund are only a first step, and China will undoubtedly make greater demands. In March 2009, China responded to uncertainty about the future role of the dollar with the revival of an old, originally French, plan from the 1960s for replacing the dollar with a synthetic reserve currency. France in the 1960s, however, was not systemically central: China today is.

Such gradual and benign adaptation is, however, difficult to achieve. Other countries need to agree to offer these additional incentives to the emerging powers. There is a danger, for example, that the United States will see that it has a unique advantage in a crisis that harms and weakens other countries. A type of rule by crisis, in which the crippled giant acts like a blinded Samson and brings down the pillars of globalization, would be an utter break with the multilateralism of the second half of the twentieth century. But such behavior is promoted by the crisis environment. And tragically, even if U.S. policymakers are not thinking like this, almost everyone else will assume that they are.

The question of whether China will respond to the new uncertainties by turning back to an increasingly state-dominated and nationalist model of development is still open. If that course is taken, the problems of deglobalization that emerged during the mid-twentieth century will follow. All the arguments from economic logic speak for continued globalization, but in sharp downturns such arguments are often trumped by a political logic that looks for conflicts and competitive advantages.

6

UNCERTAINTY OF VALUES

FINANCIAL CRISES are the catalyst for turning the globalization cycle. In such crises, assessments of the future, which form the basis of monetary valuations, change very quickly. An inability to put a correct price on an asset leads to the breakdown of markets and the erosion of confidence. Banks, businesses, and even individuals no longer trust each other. The effect on social cohesion is devastating. Collapsing values also have a spillover effect, which intensifies the process of disintegration: they fundamentally change immaterial values as well. Hence the globalization collapse becomes a story of changing values in both the usual senses of the term, as monetary and ideal values are shaken.[1]

The consequence is profound vulnerability. Trust depends on a wide range of institutional arrangements, on states, on corporations, but both governments and business become vulnerable when values change abruptly and unexpectedly. At the 2009 London G-20 summit, world leaders confirmed their need to reinstate trust when they asserted "the desirability of a new global consensus on the key values and principles that will promote sustainable economic activity."[2]

The breakdown of globalization in the past was associated with financial crises and a shifting of the geopolitical balance. Financial flows are closely correlated with the geography of power: a powerful country attracts capital, and it is also able to reexport this capital in a way that bolsters its international position. Small-scale financial crises may strengthen the link between security and dominance of the capital markets; but large-scale crises lead to a breakdown of this connection. Smaller-scale events, like 1929, may look very dramatic, but they do have easy and obvious policy answers. The catastrophic meltdown, of which the historical twentieth-century case was 1931, does not have such readily available solutions.

The connections between finance and the character of power and authority work not just at a level of high politics and the arcane calculations of security experts. They also influence the way in which people think about the myriad connections that link people across long distances and make possible the globalization phenomenon.

Complex transactions and relations in a globalized society and economy require an element of certainty that is provided by a simple capacity to make equivalences. The most obvious form of this security is the stability provided by an unwavering monetary standard. In fact, globalization upswings have always occurred in the context of a widely recognized and shared international measure of value. The late nineteenth century was characterized by Charles de Gaulle in retrospect as the *époque du trois pour cent:* the absolute confidence that government and other high-quality bonds would produce a stable and predictable return of 3 percent. The foundational belief is that market prices send an intelligible signal, and that signal has political implications. Markets have limited the capacity of governments to behave badly. Consequently, in the late twentieth century, price stability could become a major policy objective. Because the experience of the twentieth century indicated that politicians could not be trusted, this task was delegated to increasingly independent central banks.

The confidence that was at the core of the globalization-related belief in universal connectedness led many people to extend credit and take larger and larger risks. In short, the expectations aroused by globalization set off credit booms, and the down-

swing of deglobalization came with the disappoint-
ment of bubbly expectations and then with financial
collapse. But the power of the markets during the
boom had eroded alternative disciplinary methods,
whether state regulation or the imposition of a complex nonstate system of authority within a corporation. After the financial crisis began, then, there was a
universal questioning of every type of value.

In credit booms, there is not necessarily a synchro-
nized upward movement of all prices. Speculative
bubbles develop in some sectors, but not everywhere.
There is further uncertainty because periods marked
by technological transformation and structural breaks
in the economy also feature dramatic shifts in the
pattern of demand. Both the bubble and the technical change mean, then, that the relations among
prices become radically unstable. And because of
this instability of prices, it is hard to find a single
guideline for judging monetary policy. In short, the
weapon that destroys a broad range of values is price
instability.

Severe financial crises of the 1931 type do their
damage by dramatically heightening monetary uncertainty, and eroding or destroying the idea of a
common way of measuring. Even technical terms like
inflation or deflation do not capture well what is hap-

pening, because values shift significantly relative to each other. When monetary uncertainty prevails, trust and confidence are destroyed. The monetary uncertainty also corrodes institutions that had previously developed in order to eliminate additional uncertainty, that is, companies that internalize some transactions or states that offer a guarantee of stability. People in these circumstances will cast around desperately, seeking some better or truer measure of value, and hence of a guide to conduct. It is often a quite futile as well as desperate quest.

The greatest tragedy of Greek antiquity, *Oedipus Tyrannus,* opens with a priest calling out to Oedipus on behalf of the pestilence-stricken city of Thebes:

> Find some deliverance for us
> By any way that god or man can show.
> We know that experience of times past gives
> strength
> To present counsel. Therefore, O greatest of
> men,
> Restore our city to life. Have a care for your
> fame.[3]

Ironically, however, the citizens of Thebes are calling for help from the man who has brought the curse to the city. In times of pestilence—or price instability—everything becomes uncertain.

A GUIDE TO MONETARY POLICY-MAKING

The question of achieving monetary stability and stability of values has been a permanent, and in reality unsolved, obsession. Yet there have been times when most people believed that it had been entirely solved. Further, at the beginning and the end of the twentieth century, it was widely assumed that the permanence and sophistication of the solution effectively also guaranteed the continuation of the globalization phenomenon. In the first case, one hundred years ago, confidence was underpinned by gold; in the more recent globalization, it depended on the power of the human intellect to solve a policy problem.

Before the First World War, stability usually meant the adoption of a currency value fixed at a specific amount of precious metal through the mechanism of the international gold standard. The gold standard brought not only a secure guide to domestic prices, in that it seemed to guarantee against the overissue of money; it also provided a stable basis on which to deal with other peoples and other countries, since the relationship of exchange rates was fixed. This certain world of the late nineteenth-century gold standard has been the subject of a great deal of nostalgia in our own less certain age. Rapid shifts in exchange rates have been responsible for many of the banking crises that erupted in Central Europe and South America in 1931, in East Asia, and then Russia and Brazil in 1997–1998, or in central Europe again in 2009. Benn Steil and Robert Litan conclude that "national currencies have become the Achilles' heel of globalization," and propose as the best long-term answer "to rid the world of unwanted currencies."[4] UNCTAD (the United Nations Conference on Trade and Development) has pleaded for a restoration of a fixed-exchange-rate regime.

But even the gold standard did not automatically ensure price stability, and eventually some economists of that past age began to argue that a paper standard might provide a superior basis for generating real stability. The most eloquent expression of this view came from the German economist and banker Karl Helfferich, who wrote the influential tract *On Money* and concluded that "pure paper money represents the logical culmination of the history of the development of money." Helfferich at the same time saw the political disadvantages of this quite logical development. The capacity of the state and of public policy to shape value would, he predicted, encourage a mobilization and a polarization of interests, on the one hand of those who might benefit from monetary depreciation, and on the other of recipients of fixed incomes, whether as wages or interest payments, who wanted an increase in the value of money. The capacity to manipulate value would lead to a new sort of class war, in which groups would form and mobilize in order to seize the levers of power that would give them the capacity of determining value. The conflict had the capacity to lead to a "complete demoralization of economic and social life," he wrote prophetically. This was not just a speculation about the future. He was thinking of the example of agrarian populists' campaign at the end of the nineteenth century, both in America and in Europe, to inflate the currency in order to reduce the oppressive burden of farm debt.[5]

By a strange irony, it turned out that Helfferich was the major architect of the most notorious (though not quite the most severe) hyperinflation of world history, that of the German Weimar Republic after the First World War. The German Great Inflation fully lived up to Helfferich's prewar prediction. In its aftermath a savage distributional conflict broke out between those who thought of themselves as inflation losers and the big industrial and financial interests that they labeled as inflation profiteers. Many commentators at the time and later linked the great monetary disorder to the destruction of civilization and stability in Germany, and to the eventual triumph of barbarism in the form of National Socialism.[6]

There were attempts to restore the gold standard after both of the twentieth-century world wars, but in an attenuated and ultimately more unstable form. The real point of these systems was that national currencies could become more stable, and value more secure, if they were fixed in relation to other countries' currency. Some powerful country had the capacity to legislate value because it issued what was interpreted as a "key currency." There was sometimes an attempt to define the currency in terms of gold, but the most important relationship was to a key currency, the British pound, or, increasingly, the U.S. dollar (see Chapter 5). Secondary financial powers frequently resented this power, and thought of the system as time-keeping by means of a broken and inaccurate watch.

After the collapse of the fixed-exchange-rate regime in the early 1970s, the previous anchors of monetary policy disappeared. By the middle of the 1970s, some central banks had begun to argue formally for replacing fixed exchange rates with a targeting system for the growth of money. This vision, popularized as monetarism, was responsible for some great successes in stabilizing expectations, notably in Germany after the middle of the 1970s, and in the United States after 1979.

Monetarism in its purest form rapidly ran into the difficulty that it was hard to find the right measure of the money supply. Since banks in practice create money by extending credit that is then deposited in other banks and used as a basis for extending further credit, financial innovation means constant uncertainty about what precisely is money and about how its supply can be measured. In addition, the monetary authorities had no control over the velocity of circulation.

The disillusion with monetary policy produced a new interest in targeting inflation rather than monetary growth. In some cases, inflation targeting grew out of an intellectual conviction that it represented a superior way of dealing with the problem of inflationary expectations. New Zealand in 1990 and Canada in 1991 adopted this approach. Some more spectacular conversions to inflation targeting occurred in the aftermath of currency crises, as previously fixed exchange rates disintegrated and policymakers looked for an alternative tool to achieve stability. In October 1992, the United Kingdom adopted an inflation target after the British pound was forced out of the European Monetary System's exchange-rate mechanism. Sweden, which experienced a similar currency crisis, also chose the same response in January 1993.

But just as there are different measures of money, there exist a wide range of possible measures of inflation. Analysts have tried to establish a measure of core inflation (a statistic that has been at the center of Federal Reserve measures since 2000, in what it terms Personal Consumption Expenditure) by removing elements from the calculation that are very volatile, such as food and energy prices. Ben Bernanke and others in 1999 argued that a measure of core Consumer Price Inflation (CPA) "helps a central bank to communicate to the public that not every shock that raises prices would lead to a permanent increase in inflation."[7] But the concept was still rather unfamiliar. In 2003 Bernanke, then a governor of the Federal Reserve, stated in a speech that many Americans considered inflation targeting "foreign, impenetrable, and possibly slightly subversive."[8] In fact, doubts increased as to whether a core Consumer Price Index, without food and energy, would really give a long-term measure that would stabilize expectations, because it is exactly these items of consumption that are bought on a daily basis and can in practice shape expectations quite radically.

At the same time, the conventional dependence on the Consumer Price Index may also be too restrictive. One of the most intense theoretical disputes over recent years was the extent to which central banks should attempt to correct or limit bubbles in asset prices when there is no corresponding rise in the general level of inflation. Asset-price rises lead to a general increase in purchasing power, because many asset-holders will use them as securities against which to borrow. Many Europeans tried to argue in recent years for the inclusion of some element to take asset-price developments into account, but this approach was largely resisted by American policymakers and academics.[9] The problem is that asset prices and consumer price inflation may move in quite different directions, as they did in the first decade of the new millennium, and that following both would produce inconsistent policy recommendations. If they tried to devise a weighted formula to account for both—a nearly impossible exercise—central banks ran the risk of no longer appearing to follow a clearly formulated policy guideline, and they might well lose credibility.

The debate about exchange rates, monetary targeting, and even index currencies was actually an old
one. Index currencies had been widely advocated during the 1920s currency dislocations, but most central
bankers turned away from the idea because prices
were too volatile and moving in different directions.
One of them, the controversial German Hjalmar
Schacht, put it in vivid terms: "To make a price index
or a combination of several indices the basis of a currency itself would be a mistake just as much as if I
tried to measure the depth of the water of the river
Rhine with a floating peg."[10]

In fact, concepts of inflation and deflation are
quite subjective, making the achievement of a publicly satisfactory definition and measurement elusive.
A striking example of the gap between perception
and calculation occurred when European governments introduced the euro as a physical currency,
with new banknotes and coins, at the beginning of
2002. Legally, the new bank notes brought no change
at all, in that the national currencies had existed as
units defined in relation to what was at first a purely
abstract currency, the euro, since 1999. But the conversion of prices from the legacy national currencies
made many people sensitive to price changes, and
there was a widespread popular belief that the euro

had produced inflation, even though there was no evidence of this in the statisticians' calculations.[11]

The confusion about monetary values is much
greater, however, in periods of very pronounced credit
expansion, and in subsequent contractions. Nowhere
is the confusion more apparent than in discussions
of the deglobalization episode of the Great Depression.

Modern economic historians generally think of
the years prior to 1929 or 1931 as being deflationary.[12]
The international monetary system, in their view, ex-
ercised a sustained deflationary effect, because the
deficit countries (the large borrowers) were forced to
contract to address the constant threat of a loss of
monetary reserves. In a self-equilibrating system,
these contractions should have been offset by expansions in the surplus (lending countries), but the
countervailing correction did not occur. Surpluses
were concentrated in just two countries, France and
the United States, and neither wanted to expand.
France thought that increased gold reserves would be
a source of political power in the international system, and the United States also did not want to per-
mit an excessive monetary expansion, because of concerns it would translate into asset price inflation and
a stock market boom. Other countries were obliged

by the "rules of the game" to follow tight monetary policies so as not to lose even more gold and foreign exchange. Food and commodity prices showed a strong downward trend from 1925.

By contrast, at the time, in the 1920s, most economists saw signs of inflation everywhere. The German economist Melchior Palyi, for instance, saw the currency basis of the gold exchange standard as a mechanism for an inflationary creation of money.[13] Lionel Robbins in Britain claimed that stable prices did not mean the absence of inflation, and that "a stationary price-level shows an absence of inflation only when production is stationary."[14] John Maynard Keynes gave the most surprising and self-critical account of the difficulty of diagnosing inflation:

> Anyone who looked at the index of prices would see no reason to suspect any material degree of inflation, whilst anyone who looked only at the total volume of bank credit and the prices of common stocks would have been convinced of the presence of an inflation actual or impending. For my part I took the view at the time that there was no inflation in the sense in which I use this term. Looking back in the light of fuller statistical information that was then available, I

believe that while there was probably no material inflation up to the end of 1927, a genuine
profit inflation developed some time between
that date and the summer of 1929.[15]

Keynes's fullest treatment of the problem of fluc-
tuations in prices and output in *The Treatise on Money*
was published in 1930, in other words between the de-
fining crisis years of the Great Depression.[16]

Later, Keynes moved away from the kind of analysis he had offered in the *Treatise*. The analysis of the
1920s as an inflationary era became more and more
confined to Austrian-school analyses, which com-
manded no respect from mainstream economists
and seemed irrelevant to contemporary discussions.[17]

ART AND VALUES

It may be easiest to interpret the process of increased
uncertainty about values by looking at a particular
asset class. One of the most illuminating and characteristic of the millennial globalization surge is the
art market, which obviously does not play any role
in any conventional measurement of consumer inflation.

Indeed, one of the most dramatic bubbles of the new millennium occurred in the art market, above all in contemporary art. For fine art overall, the most widely quoted index, the Mei Moses index, showed an annual rise of around 20 percent over a five-year period. Art suddenly appeared to be an excellent investment, and art fairs and auctions proliferated. This particular bubble demonstrates very clearly the link between monetary values and other values. Art became important both as a speculative asset and as a statement about taste. The capacity of art possessions to make a statement about the owner's discernment was at the heart of the appeal of art as an investment category.

In the middle of the financial meltdown of September 2008, a cultural event occurred in London. While the City of London was shaken by the collapse of Lehman Brothers and the run on HBOS, Sotheby's staged a record-breaking auction for the works of the artist Damien Hirst, which produced a gross take of around $200 million. Compared with the values that were being destroyed on Wall Street, this was small change; but it was a remarkable vote of confidence in the work of one artist. Hirst was increasingly overextending himself as a result of the appetite of the market. Indeed, a few days after the September sale, he lamented, "I don't have enough time at the moment. I don't even do my own paintings."[18]

In the same way as an era of financial globalization can be summed up in the life of one fraudulent trickster, as Ivar Kreuger retrospectively incarnated the Great Depression and Bernard Madoff the boom and collapse of the twenty-first century's first decade, it is also possible to see the cycle of boom and bust reflected in a particular creative personality. In 1992, Hirst's installation *God* sold for £4,000. Six years later it was resold at £170,000. In June 2007, an installation called *Lullaby Spring*, a large metal pillbox with 6,136 pills, sold at auction for £8,600,000, over double its estimate.

Why did so many buyers want to acquire the works of Hirst at such extreme prices, and why was the dramatic reputational bubble such an additional source of attraction? Financial bubbles, like the one that was just definitively bursting at the time of the Hirst auction, are intimately related to the world of art. Renaissance Florence depended on the patronage of the Medici.[19] Sixteenth-century Venice turned the wealth of the spice trade into the canvases of Titian and Tintoretto. The world's next great commercial center was Amsterdam, where again the successful burghers pushed for a new style of art and produced the age of Rembrandt. The great nineteenth- and early twentieth-century financiers, men like J. P. Morgan, Henry Frick, and Andrew Mellon, spent a large part of their fortunes on art.

From their viewpoint, collecting art was not simply a matter of benevolence or public spiritedness. Nor was it simply a very expensive hobby. Their galleries showed in a very public way the discernment and judgment on which their financial business depended. The choice of subject, the materials, the care of execution, all acted as a signal. At the time of the Renaissance, private collections were sufficient to establish a reputation for sophisticated taste; by the late nineteenth and twentieth centuries, there was a substantial pressure to make the collector's discernment apparent to a wider public through loans or gifts to museums.

Financial judgment, by contrast, is not by its nature open to inspection. It depends on inside deals, on the market's moving ahead. It is impossible to tell who is making good bets and who is gambling recklessly. It is unwise to rely solely on the charm or persuasive capacity of the financial intermediary. Consequently, it is helpful to have a proxy activity that enables outsiders to see that the process of discernment and valuation really occurs. Of course art is not the only way of revealing supposed financial skill: it might also be a taste in fine wines (which developed also as an asset class), or skill at card games. Much of Wall Street was gripped by a poker mania in the 1980s, while the senior management at Bear Stearns was apparently appointed because of sustained skill at playing bridge. Art collecting similarly reveals a capacity for precisely conducting long-term valuations.

The recent era of global finance—maybe we can already think of it as being past—differed from the financial surge of a century ago. Its cultural manifestations also appeared to be novel. It was playful, allusive, edgy—in short, postmodern. It treated tradition and history not as a constraint, but as a source of ironic reference. A postmodern neglect or disdain for reality generated the sense that the whole world was constantly shifting and malleable, and might be as transient and meaningless as stock quotations.

To some of its participants, collecting contemporary art showed how finance had become much more of a creative process than it was during previous generations. Morgan or Mellon collected largely old masters from the cinquecento, whose reputation was clearly and solidly established. The new art collectors, however, were more like the Medici: they were really stimulating new cultural creation. As with their investments, the habitués of contemporary art markets relied not purely on their own judgment, but also on teams of sophisticated advisers and dealers who could give opinions on what trends best caught the spirit of the age.

Naive outsiders found the world of contemporary art bewildering. Why was a cow preserved in formaldehyde a great cultural achievement? What did the sheets of cloth covered by regularly interspersed colored dots—the products of Hirst's large and mechanized workshops—have to do with artistic innovation or originality?

But was not this incomprehensible quality characteristic of the increasingly sophisticated financial products that were being traded? Indeed, the nature of the risks involved was not clear, it seems, even to regulators or the senior management of the firms that were building the business.

Some modern artists and their patrons explicitly point to the parallel between contemporary art and new financial products. In both cases a fundamentally unintelligible product was being marketed to a wide audience. For example, a director of Deutsche Bank, Europe's most prominent art-collecting bank, explained a new project (called *Moment*) by say-ing that *"Moment* mirrors developments in the increasingly virtual banking business as well as tendencies in contemporary art." The bank also published the view of academic experts to the effect that customers, the broad public, were "extremely conservative, boring, lack imagination, and don't know their own minds." Customers faced by avant-garde art, or buying complex derivatives, were thus in a fundamentally similar situation, and could not understand the underlying value.[20]

After financial implosions, such as the collapse of the dot-com bubble in 2000 or the subprime meltdown of 2007–2008, such views appear arrogant. George Soros acutely saw in the postmodern and anti-Enlightenment stance a disregard for truth that allowed "the manipulation of reality to go unhindered."[21] The parallel between bewildering and apparently meaningless art and unintelligible financial products is damning rather than reassuring.

So why was the 2008 Hirst auction such a success? In part because the art involved was far from being unintelligible. The most eagerly anticipated item, a bull with golden horns and hooves, was entitled, with an obvious intent directed against the financial clients, *The Golden Calf.*

But there was another motive driving the bidders. One hint was that Russian buyers paid the big money, at the very moment that Russia's banking system was melting down. Another is the fact that at the same time there was a surge in demand for gold jewelry. The search for nonfinancial assets looks like characteristic behavior in any financial crisis—what was known during the great drama of hyperinflation in Weimar Germany as "die Flucht in die Sachwerte," the flight to material assets. In other words, art also functions as a store of value. But in order to be sure of the reliability of this function, the purchaser must be convinced of the long-term valuation of the object of desire.

The bankers of the Italian Renaissance bought works of art in part because the works reminded them of timeless values that transcended quotidian transactions. They saw their acquisitions of paintings and sculptures as a connection to eternity. Who can say the same for the products of Damien Hirst? Art had become a precise reflection of the world of rapid shifts, fast-expanding bubbles, and vertiginous collapses. It was a measure of how quickly its consumers adapted to a continually unstable and fluid economy and to rapidly evolving perceptions of reality.

ARE WE EXPERIENCING INFLATION
OR DEFLATION?

The peculiar debate of the 1920s, in which participants found it hard to say whether they were living through inflation or deflation, has an analogue in the uncertainties of the 2000s. By 2009, in an atmosphere that is unambiguously deeply deflationary, many commentators (especially from the right) are warning about inflationary or even hyperinflationary consequences of large budget deficits and of central bank monetary accommodation of those deficits. Since deflation and inflation are generally taken to refer to broad general or overall movements of prices, it is easy to see how rapid price shifts can produce conceptual confusion regarding the application of these central terms of monetary analysis.

The current debate had a much milder anticipation in 2002–2003, when interest rates were low and there was a fear that the deflationary Japanese experience of the 1990s might be repeated more widely. At that time, in a reassuring speech in which deflation was presented as a very remote possibility indeed, Bernanke argued, "Deflation is in almost all cases a side effect of a collapse of aggregate demand—a drop in spending so severe that producers must cut prices on an ongoing basis in order to find buyers." The most famous passage of the speech took up an old idea of Milton Friedman's: "A money-financed tax cut is essentially equivalent to Milton Friedman's famous 'helicopter drop' of money."[22] The aim was to show that deflation was impossible—but how could anyone be sure?

The stability of price and wage expectations surprised some analysts in an era in which there were high rates of money growth and many signs of asset price inflation. In 2006 the Bank for International Settlements argued that "relatively easy policies have continued to allow the build-up of a host of financial 'imbalances' that are becoming increasingly dangerous as time passes."[23] Japan's attempt to stem deflation through a lowering of interest rates and monetary expansion did not affect Japanese prices, but it did induce inflation (especially in asset prices) elsewhere, as borrowing in yen produced a booming "carry trade." But no one wanted to sound an alarm bell about the monetary expansion, because many prices were not rising. The most usual explanation was that the combination of a stability-oriented monetary policy with the extension of manufacturing production over the world was exercising a steady downward push on prices. This might even generate an "end of inflation."[24]

A more powerful explanation tried to distinguish good and bad deflations. Bad deflations were the type familiar from the Great Depression, and followed from financial-sector instability. Good deflation was a consequence of technical change, and the lowering of prices (as well as the phenomenon of improved quality) reflected not just economic globalization but above all the power of technical innovation. This story, relived in the early twenty-first century, had been a hallmark of the most dynamic periods of nineteenth-century economic growth. Prices and profits fell, but consumers had more choice and were much better off.[25]

The possibility of "good deflation" helps to explain why the deflation issue has generated so much confusion. But the confusion is deeper, because the periods of transition and innovation feature all kinds of change that contemporaries want to bring into some kind of logical association with each other. An insightful Austrian commentator wrote at the end of 1931, the most crisis-filled year of the Great Depression: "Wartime destruction and military orders, blockade and inflation, the destruction of old states, the creation of new political machineries, technical revolutions in industry and agriculture, social and moral revolutions, new ways of behaving, new sexual morality, new eating habits, new female clothes, a new relationship with nature, new sports: never in economic history have so many sources of disturbance of such profound impact coincided as over the last decade."[26]

In each transition from one sort of economic structure to another, from agriculture to manufacturing in the mid-nineteenth century, or in the crisis of manufacturing in the 1930s, the change was marked by dramatic price declines that fundamentally follow from innovation. In addition, today we have a particular problem. Our innovation has been concentrated in the financial sector (see Chapter 4). But financial activity is especially vulnerable to deflation as a result of uncertainty and the collapse of trust. A massive deleveraging is now occurring as part of the process of a new type of pernicious deflation, and that is not really comparable to the slow and very mild Japanese stagnation of the 1990s (where annual price declines rarely exceeded 1 percent), or to the worries about deflation in 2002–2003.

The year 2008 started with ripples from the subprime crisis that generated considerable nervousness.

There were signs of recession in the industrial countries, especially in the United States and Britain, as house prices fell. But there were also signs of worrying inflation as commodity prices surged. As the markets closed before American Independence Day, on July 3, a barrel of West Texas intermediate petroleum was priced at $145.30. The indicators seemed to suggest a long bout of stagflation, with historical parallels to the 1970s.

The second half of the year produced even grimmer parallels. The mood became more millenarian as we passed from fire to ice with the vanishing of the inflationary flame. By the end of the year, a barrel of West Texas oil was more than $100 cheaper than it had been at its Independence Day peak. New parallels were made to the 1930s, and to the sustained experience of debt deflation. Instead of recollections of Heath and Wilson, or Nixon and Carter, people started to think of Ramsay MacDonald and Herbert Hoover, or of Germany's unfortunate chancellor Heinrich Brüning, who presided over the deflation that destroyed the Weimar Republic. To some, even the 1930s sounded too benign. The deputy governor of the Bank of England in late October called the situation the "largest financial crisis of its kind in human history."[27]

Deflation and inflation are both monetary processes. In consequence people mistakenly assume they are fundamentally similar, and that they can be controlled by the operation of the same policy instruments, employed in opposite directions.

Inflation requires monetary restraint, and a period of tightening interest rates. Financial history celebrates the heroes who killed inflation. In the first half of the twentieth century, there was the German Hjalmar Schacht, who mastered the Weimar Republic's hyperinflation of the early 1920s and became the savior of Weimar democracy before he turned into the more sinister shape of Adolf Hitler's financial wizard. The most legendary American central banker of all time is a much more benign figure. Paul Volcker killed the inflation of the Nixon and Carter years, and now, at age eighty-one, is again back at the center of policy-making as one of Barack Obama's key advisers.

Deflation, if it is seen as a precise mirror image of inflation, should also be quite easy to deal with. That is the implication of the famous helicopter analogy. The challenge requires simply the remedy of cutting interest rates . . . and then cutting them further. The Bank of England, the Federal Reserve, and the European Central Bank have engaged in interest-rate reductions, both on their own as well as in coordinated moves to impress the markets. The markets were impressed, for about a day in each case, and then the panic resumed. The deflationary expectations had become very deeply embedded because of the weakness of financial institutions.

Another way to meet the challenge of deflation—or so the common thinking goes—is through monetary expansion and the provision of more liquidity to the financial system . . . and then by providing more liquidity. In late 2007, this strategy worked well. In 2008 it did not. The major central banks injected over $2.5 trillion, and again produced a temporary calm, but could not inspire banks to resume normal lending. By 2009, some major central banks, notably the Federal Reserve and the Bank of England, went over to purchases of long-term assets in order to affect the term structure of interest rates, and not simply the short end of the market, in what was called nonconventional monetary policy. As this policy evolved, there was little discussion of how the volume of assets purchased in this way was linked to estimates of the future likely behavior of inflation.

Or finally, the deflationary threat could be managed by having central banks or governments buy up bad assets. That might have been a better solution, and it was the central plank of the plan by Treasury Secretary Hank Paulson, and then in Secretary Timothy Geithner's revised version. But it proved too complicated, because the bad debts were not simple or homogenous financial instruments (as were, for example, the debts of Latin American countries in the 1980s debt crisis). Each of the bad assets was bad in a unique way and needed to be individually priced. This pricing exercise proved simply too complicated to be managed expeditiously in a crisis setting.

Something in this story of a futile fight against deflation gives us pause. And so does the historical record. There are no antideflationary heroes equivalent to Volcker. It is extraordinarily difficult to emerge successfully from deflation, and the sustained episodes of the United States in the 1930s or Japan in the 1990s were not followed by a lasting recovery. Monetary stabilization may occur, but the beneficial consequences are in large part impeded by the political response to the deflationary predicament. Full employment in the United States returned only as a result of the Second World War. While people and policies can be the heroes in dealing with inflation, the best hope in the long run for overcoming deflation is technical innovation and the increased spending power that it creates.

But in the meantime, people will react strongly against the order that is driving down values. Deflation emanating from the financial sector is especially lethal. First, it is simply more difficult to deal with than inflation for technical reasons. Interest rates can be reduced to zero, and indeed it is conceivable that a negative interest rate could be implemented so that the central bank would charge us to keep our money safe.

But the closer to zero that interest rates fall, the more problematic monetary policy becomes. The policy instruments do not seem to work, and the measurements indicate weird figures. Central bankers become like pilots flying into the Bermuda Triangle and finding that their altimeters and speedometers simply do not appear to be giving reliable readings. As they look down at their control panel, central bankers see the monetary base in Britain, the United States, or the Eurozone growing by incredibly large figures. In October 2008, the U.S. monetary base increased by 25 percent and in November by 27 percent. Taken by themselves, numbers like this might look like the indicators of a new inflation rather than of deflation.

The "zero boundary" for interest rates prompts some ingenious answers. In 1931 in a small Austrian mountain town called Wörgl, the municipality introduced "disappearing money." Bank notes required the fixing of a gummed stamp every month in order to maintain their validity. It might be conceivable to replicate this idea to stop bank-note hoarding with more sophisticated technical means, say by installing on a banknote chips that require periodic reloading.

There is a further and more profound reason that deflation is such a threat, and that policymakers setting out to eliminate the deflation dragon have a much tougher task than the inflation fighters: all prices do not move down, and in particular, debts do not adjust because they are fixed in nominal terms. It is this that produces the weird reading of the cockpit instruments.

Inflation and deflation of debts produce very different outcomes. Inflation reduces the value of debt, and creates a nice buzz of light-headed excitement as people and companies are unburdened. For many people, this is like slowly sipping champagne. Deflation, by contrast, increases debt, and feels like being smothered by a lead blanket. In the interwar Great Depression, in a famous analysis, the economist Irving Fisher accurately described the process of debt deflation, in which lenders worried by the deterioration of their asset quality called in their loans, pushing borrowers to liquidate assets further, and continue to drive down prices, all of which led to new credit-cutting as well as bankruptcies and bank failures.[28] The statist response was a very characteristically twentieth-century response to the new uncertainty.

The assumption of debt by the state is the answer that corresponds to the current rhetorical consensus appearing in the speeches of President Obama, President Sarkozy, or Prime Minister Gordon Brown, that finance should be the servant and not the master of the economy. Such statements echo very precisely the sentiments expressed by politicians, both democratic and nondemocratic, of the Great Depression. Does the taking over of debt by the state solve the economic problem? Not necessarily, because it does not inevitably restart a flow of funds to productive or dynamic sectors of the economy. Does it solve the moral problem of debt?

LOOKING FOR NEW SOLUTIONS

There are also signs today of a much older answer to deflation and its tendency to enhance the level and burden of debt. Deflation produces radical anticapitalism, and a demand for a cancellation of debt. Revulsion against the market economy often takes the form of a specific condemnation of debt and debt instruments. The Saudi cleric Grand Mufti Abdul Aziz Al-Sheikh made the case that the cause of the crisis is interest on debt, and that the *sharia* principle of risk participation would eliminate the problem. This is a very old answer. The Old Testament famously recommended a cancellation of debt every forty-nine years in a "jubilee." The medieval church attacked usury. Such arguments are not built on simple obscurantism. Both the medieval church and Islam distinguish between debt that is exploitative, in which individuals are tied in debt servitude, and the relationship that arises out of a sharing of entrepreneurial risk. The old answers invite us to think about the circumstances in which debt may inhibit free choice, or the free development of the human personality.

These answers see debt as producing a fundamental moral flaw. Today debt is much more prominent than it was in medieval Europe. Consumers in advanced industrial countries (and in particular the United States) rely on debt in order to buy. Treasury Secretary Paulson complained that the credit crunch was "making it more expensive for families to finance everyday purchases."[29] But dependence on debt polarizes societies. Bailout proposals run into opposition from those who are not so highly indebted, and who see an overall solution as a subsidy for the improvident.

The theological interpretation of modernity is that we borrow from one another on an increasingly grand scale for a reason, and that that reason stands as a condemnation of modern life. We borrow because we are convinced that our utility schedule is more important than someone else's. If I see a beautiful piece of jewelry or a bright new car in a shop, I am convinced that it should be mine and that it can be more usefully employed in my possession than in that of someone else. In that way greed feeds on a kind of pride or self-regard. The problematic character of debt is captured in an ambiguous phrase of the Lord's Prayer that refers not only to spiritual offense but also to actual debt (and was often in the past translated as "forgive us our debts," *dimitte nobis debita nostra*).

The financial crisis has produced a massive increase in the demand for religious answers to insoluble secular problems. Economists analyzed the increase in church attendances as a response to the recession. At the World Economic Forum in 2008, the founder of this annual gathering of influential globalizers, Klaus Schwab, told his audience that it was time to "pay for the sins of the past." The U.S. literary critic Stanley Fish touted the seventeenth-century Anglican metaphysical poet George Herbert as offering the best response to the problem of debt and guilt. "This economy, in which funds depleted are endlessly replenished, is underwritten by a power so great and beneficent that it turns failures into treasures. Some economists identify that power as the market and ask us to have faith in it. God might be a better candidate." British prime minister Gordon Brown told the Scottish Labour Party: "We believe that markets need not just money men but morals, that being fair matters far more than being laissez-faire and that banks must always serve the public, not themselves."[30]

The meltdown of capitalism produced a big blame game both in the 1930s, when industrial capitalism broke down, and today, when it is financially driven capitalism that has gone wrong. Today the collapse is widely thought to be the responsibility of inept regulators and monetary policymakers, unscrupulous mortgage originators, or greedy banks. Popular commentators like to go back to stereotypes from earlier eras, such as the figure of Gordon Gekko in Oliver Stone's movie *Wall Street*, who memorably proclaimed that "Greed is good."

The attributions of blame do not contemplate why

a little bit of greed can produce such bad effects. Greed works as a doctrine of management because it is endlessly replicated in everyday behavior, by neighbors who borrow because they want to match other people's consumption patterns, or buy bigger houses out of a competitive spirit. Wall Street moved prices by means of a "thundering herd," but it is not the only locus of greed. We might equally look to popular culture, to game shows, or to shopping behavior. In November 2008, the same instincts that drove financial markets produced the post-Thanksgiving consumption-intoxicated herd that trampled a store clerk to death in a Long Island Wal-Mart.

It may be depressing to conclude that there are no immediate fixes to a disaster of the 1931 type, or that institutional weaknesses reflect basic problems of human conduct and motivation. Solutions to the crisis include a simplification of finance, a return to lower levels of debt, and a reduction of flows of capital across long distances. The quasi-nationalization of banks is already producing some of these effects, in that the new government-owned institutions are unlikely to be willing to let their funds flow across national frontiers, where they would be used to the benefit of citizens of a different political entity. Sometimes this package is discussed as a move to "retro finance."[31]

An alternative direction involves considering measures that would increase confidence. There might be a more direct relationship of individuals to financial activity, one that leaves them more empowered and does not place them in the hands of people whom they do not and cannot trust. But trust is not something that can simply be created at will by governments or ordered by legislative fiat. Trust depends on a delicate social infrastructure. It is also intrinsically related to a capacity for empathy or sympathy, the capacity to put oneself in the perspective of another when contemplating a business transaction. This is a tradition of thought that on the one hand derives from Adam Smith's reflections in the *Theory of the Moral Sentiments,* and on the other from religious thinking about compassion or misericordia. But it has been largely marginalized because of the development of powerful institutions, corporations, and state regulations that seemed to obviate the need for a moral imagination.[32]

The projection of moral thought into business relations runs against a powerful stream of recent thinking, in which financial thinking detached itself from the rest of the world and became a sort of mathematical abstraction. One of the most reflective and self-critical modern masters of finance, George Soros, once wrote: "If I had to deal with people instead of markets, I could not have avoided moral choices and I could not have been so successful in making money. I blessed the luck that led me to the financial markets and allowed me not to dirty my hands."[33]

At this stage, there arises the most fundamental problem in regard to values in economics. Many analysts have suggested that a market society cannot live simply on the basis of the values that it generates itself as a result of its own commercial activities and exchanges. The fundamental values derive from some other source. A powerful current of interpretation suggests a religious origin of such basic values regarding human dignity, human motivation, and conduct. In a famous tract, Max Weber tried to suggest that the ethic that drove modern capitalism had originated with a cultivation of a very unbusinesslike asceticism in the world of the Reformation. The idea of renunciation and a denial of consumption then produced an accumulation of surpluses. The initial asceticism of the business elite gradually eroded as it was replaced by what Weber called the "iron cage" of rationalistic calculation. The original motivation disappeared, generating, according to Weber's account, a feeling of emptiness.

Conduct in a market society needs to be guided by some external source of commonly defined and commonly held values. If those values erode, instability ensues. Globalization does not automatically establish a self-sustaining set of values. On the contrary, the continual change and uncertainty that accompany globalization, driven by new encounters, new possibilities, and new technologies, tend to subvert this process. A crisis then produces the demand for a return to older values. In the current circumstances, there is even nostalgia for the Weberian conception of a Protestant work ethic. At his inauguration in January 2009, President Obama spoke of American greatness: "In reaffirming the greatness of our nation, we understand that greatness is never a given. It must be earned. Our journey has never been one of shortcuts or settling for less. It has not been the path for the faint-hearted, for those who prefer leisure over work, or seek only the pleasures of riches and fame."[34] The President of the United States appeared to be explicitly setting aside the late twentieth-century obsession with happiness and the measurement of "pleasures" as a way of judging the value of economic activity. It coincided happily with the themes of Asian frugality and Asian values that framed an attack on American hegemony by the governor of the People's Bank of China. Zhou Xiaochuan emphasized the importance of Confucianism, which values "thrift, self-discipline, Middle Ground and anti-extravagancy."[35] But such appeals still raise the Weberian question of how and why the work ethic motivates us.

Since the Industrial Revolution, three developments have made the classical modern institutional answer to the recurring problem of trust in economic transactions—namely the corporation as regulated by a sovereign state—more and more problematic. First, globalized business is not confined to national frontiers. So which regulators are responsible and which sets of rules should be obeyed? Second, innovative businesses are often good at anticipating and circumventing attempts at regulation: especially in financial services, there is a constant race between regulatory responses to perceived problems and innovation that makes the regulation obsolete or inappropriate. And third, the character and structure of a company are constantly changing with new technologies (especially information technology) and are as a consequence less subject to hierarchical control. Taken together, all these developments make the idea that a particular sort of institutionalized corporate culture can by itself produce good behavior ever more debatable.

The question of the citizenship of business corporations became deeply problematic over the twentieth century, because they were increasingly operating across national boundaries. The idea that a responsible multinational or transnational corporation should aim to be a good citizen not just in its country of origin but also in the host countries in which it operates is expressed over and over again by anxious executives.

These questions have an additional special urgency because of the regulatory "arms" race in which each new attempt at regulation soon produces as a response a technology that makes the regulation obsolete and prompts further and new regulatory action. So in the more mundane setting of day-to-day decisions, businesses often cannot have any significant or effective guidance from governments because the subject matter is too complex. And correspondingly, governments and regulators for some time felt obliged to rely on banks' self-enforced and even self-formulated standards. This problem is well understood in some technical areas, such as the regulation and supervision of financial-sector risk, where a modern international consensus has left large parts of regulation to the banks' own risk models, with disastrous consequences. But it applies equally in areas where businesses need to make judgments about the kind of government they are dealing with when they extend their operations globally: should companies ignore poor human rights records that may be responsible for some of the attractions (reduced labor costs) of a particular production location?

The complex hierarchical structures of classical companies as they developed in the nineteenth century, with layers of management controlling and transmitting instructions to inferior layers, while information was passed up the other way, have become much flatter. In large part, this is the result of improved information technology, which makes the control function of the classical company easier to implement. It is easy for technology to supply up-to-date sales information, and for the central executives to respond immediately: they no longer need the buffer of an enormous management hierarchy. But there is also much more room for autonomous action at all levels of the business. The emphasis on flexibility and independence allows greater possibilities for entrepreneurial action, but it also frequently makes it impossible for top management to understand what is going on throughout the corporation. This is especially the case in highly complex transnational structures such as Citigroup, which at the height of its fortunes had branches in over a hundred countries, or AIG, which was active in 130 countries.

Changing philosophies have also played a significant role in the flattening of the corporate hierarchy. Especially the popularization of agency theory has led individual businesspeople to internalize a mode of analysis as a norm for behavior.[36] It looks like an appealing model for understanding a world in which corporations are in flux, and ownership, markets, technologies are constantly changing.

The remodeling of the corporation, as well as a new self-understanding of behavior within the enterprise, makes for a greater vulnerability to reputational risk. In the absence of very clear hierarchies, and with much more initiative and responsibility delegated to distant and junior employees, it is much easier for a company to be crippled or its reputation damaged by the action of a single employee. It may be a question of inappropriate financial risk, combined with unauthorized and dishonest behavior in order to alleviate the consequences of that risk, as in the case of the old London banking house of Barings, which was brought down by the actions of a Singapore manager, Nick Leeson. It may be an issue of catastrophic negligence, as in the oil spill of the *Exxon Valdez,* or the Texas oil refinery explosions of British Petroleum. In the more recent scandals, in Bear Stearns, Lehman Brothers, or AIG, there are more obvious coordination failures at the very top of the enterprise. In all these cases, apparently isolated examples of bad behavior have profound effects on corporations that have a global reach. Indeed, the failure of a corporate ethic brought down the model of financial globalization.

Cases such as these demonstrate the need for an ethic of personal responsibility that cannot simply be subsumed in some vague sense of corporate culture. A recent study of the operation of scientific research concluded that the advance of science depended on complicated systems of trust among colleagues that were built by "communities of virtue."[37] Ethical questions have become again absolutely central to a firm's reputation, and to its ability to do business. We are back in a world in which trust is a virtue that is required as a logical precondition of being an effective participant in markets.

Globalization depends on being able to achieve and maintain trust over long distances, between strangers, and in situations that are full of legal uncertainty. The increased emphasis on the state and its role in regulating business activity is likely to produce new conflicts and clashes, and to heighten the level of uncertainty. In the world of globalization, many people make assumptions about common values, but these are often not articulated fully, and when they are articulated, they frequently provoke a fierce reaction. The only way of dealing with a collapse in values is to rebuild values. When there is deep distress, as in the case of Oedipus, there is no easy answer. Regaining trust is a long and arduous process. That is why when globalization is broken, it is not easy to put together again. We will look for communities of virtue, but inevitably we will not find them at once. And the globalization cycle will resume, but not immediately.

NOTES

INDEX

NOTES

Introduction

1. Ken Livingstone at http://news.bbc.co.uk/2/hi/
   indepth/uk_politics/2000/london_mayor/
   709266.stm (accessed December 1, 2008).
2. See my book *The End of Globalization* (Cambridge:
   Harvard University Press, 2001).
3. Quoted in "Fat Cats in Terror," *Daily Mail* (London), March 26, 2009.
4. J. H. Plumb, *The Growth of Political Stability in England: 1675–1725* (London: Macmillan, 1967).

1. The End of Globalization

1. See, for example, Kevin H. O'Rourke and Jeffrey G.
   Williamson, *Globalization and History: The Evolution
   of a Nineteenth-Century Atlantic Economy* (Cambridge:
   MIT Press, 1999).
2. Ronald Findlay and Kevin H. O'Rourke, *Power and
   Plenty: Trade, War, and the World Economy in the Second
   Millennium* (Princeton, N.J.: Princeton University
   Press, 2008).

3. Michael Bordo, book review in *Finance and Development* 39, no. 1 (March 2002).

4. Wilfrid Ward, ed., *Newman's Apologia Pro Vita Sua* (1864; London: Oxford University Press, 1913), pp. 336–337.

5. Etienne Balibar, "Strangers as Enemies: Further Reflections on the Aporias of Globalization," Globalization working paper 06/4, McMaster University, Canada, May 2006, http://globalization.mcmaster .ca/wps/balibar.pdf (accessed April 22, 2009); Hans-Ulrich Obrist, "Die Polyphonie der Zentren," in Henning Schulte-Noelle and Michael M. Thoss, eds., *Abendland unter? Reden über Europa* (Munich: Diederichs/Hugendubel, 2007), p. 211.

6. Robert Howse, "The End of the Globalization Debate: A Review Essay," *Harvard Law Review* 121 (2008): 1528–1554.

7. See Joseph Stiglitz, *Globalization and Its Discontents* (New York: W. W. Norton, 2002); and Ulrich Beck, *Macht und Gegenmacht im globalen Zeitalter* (Frankfurt: Suhrkamp, 2002), esp. pp. 416–418.

8. See Surjit S. Bhalla, *Imagine There's No Country: Poverty, Inequality, and Growth in the Era of Globalization* (Washington, D.C.: Institute for International Economics, 2002).

9. Michael Bordo and Barry Eichengreen, "Crises Now and Then: What Lessons from the Last Era of Financial Globalization," in Paul Mizen, ed., *Monetary*

History, Exchange Rates and Financial Markets: Essays in Honor of Charles Goodhart, vol. 2 (London: Edward Elgar, 2003), pp. 52–91.

10. See Jorge Castaneda, "Latin America's Left Turn," *Foreign Affairs* 85, no. 3 (May–June 2006).

11. In practice this new politics was worked out by Bodo Hombach and Peter Mandelson. See the Schröder-Blair paper "The Way Forward for Europe's Social Democrats," June 8, 1999, published in German as "Der Weg nach vorn für Europas Sozialdemokraten," *Blätter für deutsche und internationale Politik* (July 1999): 887–896.

12. Ulrich Beck, "Warum Europa," in Schulte-Noelle and Thoss, *Abendland unter? Reden über Europa,* p. 188.

13. The concept obtained widespread circulation in September 2007 in a report by Jim O'Neill of Goldman Sachs. See O'Neill, "The Changing World," *Global Economics Weekly* 7, no. 29 (September 5, 2007).

14. Patrick Low, *Trading Free: The GATT and U.S. Trade Policy* (New York: Twentieth Century Fund Press, 1995), p. 247.

15. Stiglitz, *Globalization and Its Discontents,* p. 130.

16. Douglas A. Irwin, *Against the Tide: An Intellectual History of Free Trade* (Princeton, N.J.: Princeton University Press, 1996), p. 19.

17. Sam Dillon, "U.S.-Mexico Study Sees Exaggeration

of Migration Data," *New York Times,* August 31, 1997, pp. A1, A6.

18. Notably Paul Krugman, "Growing World Trade: Causes and Consequences," *Brookings Papers on Economic Activity* 25 (1995): 327-362.

19. See Paul Samuelson, "Where Ricardo and Mill Rebut and Confirm Mainstream Economists Supporting Globalization," *Journal of Economic Perspectives* 18, no. 3 (2004); Alan Blinder, "Fear of Offshoring," working paper no. 119, Princeton University Center for Economic Policy Studies, December 16, 2005; and "Offshoring: the Next Industrial Revolution?" *Foreign Affairs* 85, no. 2 (March–April 2006): 113-128.

20. Philip T. Hoffman, Gilles Postel-Vinay, and Jean-Laurent Rosenthal, *Surviving Large Losses: Financial Crises, the Middle Class, and the Development of Capital Markets* (Cambridge: Belknap Press of Harvard University Press, 2007).

21. Déclaration de M. Nicolas Sarkozy, Président de la République, sur les mesures de soutien à l'économie face à la crise économique internationale, à Argonay (Haute-Savoie) le 23 octobre 2008, http://discours.vie-publique.fr/notices/087003350.html (accessed April 22, 2009).

22. Robert H. Frank, *Luxury Fever: Money and Happiness in an Era of Excess* (Princeton, N.J.: Princeton University Press, 1999).

23. Richard Layard, *Happiness: Lessons from a New Science* (New York: Penguin, 2005).

24. British Cabinet Office, "Life Satisfaction: The State of Knowledge and Implications for Government," http://www.cabinetoffice.gov.uk/media/cabinetoffice/strategy/assets/paper.pdf (accessed April 22, 2009).

25. Peter Evans, "The Eclipse of the State? Reflections on Stateness in an Era of Globalization," *World Politics* 50, no. 1 (1997): 62–89; Andrew Hurrell, *On Global Order* (Oxford, Eng.: Oxford University Press, 2007), p. 201.

26. Vito Tanzi and Ludger Schuknecht, *Public Spending in the Twentieth Century: A Global Perspective* (Cambridge, Eng.: Cambridge University Press, 2000).

27. Dani Rodrik, *Has Globalization Gone Too Far?* (Washington, D.C.: Institute for International Economics, 1997).

28. Frederic S. Mishkin, *The Next Great Globalization: How Disadvantaged Nations Can Harness Their Financial Systems to Get Rich* (Princeton, N.J.: Princeton University Press, 2006).

2. Which Historical Analogy Applies?

1. See Douglas Diamond and Phillip Dybvig, "Bank Runs, Liquidity, and Deposit Insurance," *Journal of Political Economy* 91 (1983): 401–419; Charles Calomiris and Gary Gorton, "The Origins of

Banking Panics: Models, Facts, and Bank Regulation," in Charles W. Calomiris, *U.S. Bank Deregulation in Historical Perspective* (Cambridge, Eng.: Cambridge University Press, 2000).

2. Knut Borchardt, *Wachstum, Krisen, Handlungsspielräume der Wirtschaftspolitik: Studien zur Wirtschaftsgeschichte des 19. und 20. Jahrhunderts* (Göttingen: Vandenhoeck & Ruprecht, 1982), p. 166.

3. John Maynard Keynes, *The General Theory of Employment, Interest, and Money* (London: Macmillan, 1936), pp. 154, 155, 159.

4. Milton Friedman and Anna J. Schwartz, *A Monetary History of the United States* (Princeton, N.J.: Princeton University Press, 1963).

5. See Michael D. Bordo, Ehsan U. Choudhri, and Anna J. Schwartz, "Could Stable Money Have Averted the Great Contraction?" *Economic Inquiry* 33, no. 3 (1995): 484–505.

6. Helmut Schmidt, "Vorsicht Finanzhaie," *Die Zeit,* October 8, 1998, p. 2.

7. George Soros, *The Crisis of Global Capitalism: Open Society Endangered* (New York: Public Affairs, 1998), pp. 103, 134. He later admitted, "I was proven wrong." George Soros, *The New Paradigm for Financial Markets: The Credit Crisis of 2008 and What It Means* (New York: Public5 Affairs, 2008), p. 99.

8. Quoted in John Authers and Gillian Tett, "Ins and

Outs of the Ups and Downs," *Financial Times,* January 25, 2008.

9. Quoted in Katharina Bart and Goran Mijuk, "In UBS Vote a Mixed Message," *Wall Street Journal,* February 28, 2008.

10. Eugene Fama, "The Behavior of Stock Market Prices," *Journal of Business* 38 (1965): 34-105. Paul Samuelson, "Proof That Properly Anticipated Prices Fluctuate Randomly," *Industrial Management Review* 6 (1965): 41-49. The theory goes back to the 1900 dissertation of Louis Bachelier, "Théorie de la Spéculation," Ecole Normale Supérieure, Paris. The most important popular presentation of the theory is Burton Malkiel's bestseller, *A Random Walk down Wall Street* (New York: Norton, 1981). See also Burton G. Malkiel, "The Efficient Market Hypothesis and Its Critics," working paper no. 91, Princeton University Center for Economic Policy Studies, 2003.

11. This was especially true for Robert J. Shiller's bestseller *Irrational Exuberance* (Princeton, N.J.: Princeton University Press, 2000), which was fortuitously published on the eve of the dot-com crash.

12. Frederick Lewis Allen, *Only Yesterday: An Informal History of the 1920s* (New York: Harper & Brothers, 1931); John K. Galbraith, *The Great Crash of 1929* (1955; Harmondsworth, Eng.: Penguin, 1975); John Brooks, *Once in Golconda: A True Drama of Wall Street,*

1920–1938 (New York: Harper & Row, 1969); Charles P. Kindleberger, *Manias, Panics, and Crashes: A History of Financial Crises* (New York: Basic Books, 1978).

13. Eugene White, "The Stock Market Boom and Crash of 1929 Revisited," *Journal of Economic Perspectives* 4, no. 2 (1990): 67–83, argues more moderately that economic data were predicting a (relatively mild) recession, and that the stock market reacted to this.

14. Peter Temin, *Did Monetary Forces Cause the Great Depression?* (New York: Norton, 1976), pp. 78–83.

15. The most explicit account of 1929 that offers this explanation is Irving Fisher, *The Stock Market Crash— And After* (New York: Macmillan, 1930).

16. "Cotton Futures Decline Sharply," *New York Times,* October 24, 1929, p. 53.

17. Paul Krugman, "Fear Itself," *New York Times Magazine,* September 30, 2001, p. 36.

18. Ben Bernanke, "The Macroeconomics of the Great Depression: A Comparative Approach," *Journal of Money Credit and Banking* 27 (February 1995): 1–28.

19. Quoted in Allen, *Only Yesterday,* p. 330; Galbraith, *Great Crash,* p. 123.

20. "Panicky Liquidation on Stock Exchange Partly Checked," *New York Times,* October 25, 1929, p. 45.

21. "Phone, Radio, Cable Beat All Records," *New York Times,* October 30, 1929, p. 3.

22. See Barry Eichengreen, *Golden Fetters: The Gold Stan-*

dard and the Great Depression, 1919–1939 (New York: Oxford University Press, 1992), p. 251.

23. Lionel Robbins, *The Great Depression* (London: Macmillan, 1934), p. 49.

24. Thomas E. Hall and J. David Ferguson, *The Great Depression: An International Disaster of Perverse Economic Policies* (Ann Arbor: University of Michigan Press, 1998), p. 66.

25. Temin, *Did Monetary Forces Cause the Great Depression?* p. 72.

26. See Ben Bernanke and Mark Gertler, "Inside the Black Box: The Credit Channel of Monetary Policy Transmission," *Journal of Economic Perspectives* 9 (Winter 1995): 27–48.

27. Galbraith, *Great Crash,* p. 147.

28. "Falls Dead at Ticker as Stocks Decline," *New York Times,* October 28, 1929, p. 3.

29. Quoted in Clive Cookson, "Bank Crises Kill, Says Study," *Financial Times,* February 26, 2008, p. 3.

30. Marek Okólski, "Demographic Processes before and during the Ongoing Transition in Poland," *International Journal of Sociology* 34, no. 4 (Winter 2004–2005): 3–37; see also Marek Okólski, *Reprodukcja ludności a modernizacja społeczeństwa: Polski syndrom* [Population Reproduction and Modernization] (Warsaw: Ksiazka i Wiedza, 1988).

31. "Heavy Break in Stocks," *New York Times,* October 24, 1929, p. 43.

32. "Breaks of the Past Recalled in Street," *New York Times,* October 25, 1929, p. 3.

33. Robert J. Shiller, "Investor Behavior in the October 1987 Stock Market Crash: Survey Evidence," National Bureau of Economic Research working paper no. 2446 (Washington, D.C.: NBER, November 1987), p. 24.

34. "The Wall Street Readjustment: Its Present Meaning and Significance for the Future," *New York Times,* October 25, 1929, p. 36.

35. Quoted in William Safire, "Fear Itself," *New York Times,* October 21, 1987, p. A35.

36. Quoted in Galbraith, *Great Crash,* p. 140.

37. Quoted in "Brokers Believe Bottom Is Reached," *New York Times,* October 30, 1929, p. 7.

38. Quoted in "Calls Stock Crash Blow at Gamblers," *New York Times,* October 29, 1929, p. 23.

39. Quoted in Galbraith, *Great Crash,* p. 128.

40. Morgenthau quoted in *United Nations Monetary and Financial Conference, Bretton Woods, New Hampshire, July 1 to July 22, 1944: Final Act and Related Documents* (Washington, D.C.: U.S. Government Printing Office, 1944), document 522; Keynes, *General Theory,* p. 159.

41. An exception is Peter Temin, "The German Crisis of 1931: Evidence and Tradition," *Cliometrica* 1 (2007): 5–17; see also Ben S. Bernanke, *Essays on the Great*

Depression (Princeton, N.J.: Princeton University Press, 2000).

42. Bradford DeLong and Lawrence H. Summers, "The Changing Cyclical Variability of Economic Activity in the United States," in Robert J. Gordon, ed., *The American Business Cycle: Continuity and Change* (Chicago: University of Chicago Press, 1986), p. 689.

43. A. J. Sherman, trans., *The Raven of Zurich: The Memoirs of Felix Somary* (London: C. Hurts & Co., 1986).

44. See Iago Gil Aguado, "The Creditanstalt Crisis of 1931 and the Failure of the Austro-German Customs Union Project," *Historical Journal* 44 (2001): 199–221.

45. Ibid., p. 201.

46. The interpretation of the German crisis as a currency crisis or a banking crisis has produced a recent historiographical controversy. For the interpretation as a currency crisis, see Thomas Ferguson and Peter Temin, "Made in Germany: The German Currency Crisis of 1931," *Research in Economic History* 21 (2003): 1–53, and Temin, "German Crisis"; for the banking crisis interpretation, see Isabel Schnabel, "The Twin German Crisis of 1931," *Journal of Economic History* 64 (2004): 822–871; also Harold James, "The Causes of the German Banking Crisis of 1931," *Economic History Review* 38 (1984): 68–87.

47. See, for example, Hans Schäffer, "Geheimgeschichte

der Bankenkrise," in Schäffer diary, ED 93/31, July 29, 1931, Institut für Zeitgeschichte, Munich.

48. Quoted in *Verhandlungen des VII: Allgemeinen Deutschen Bankiertages zu Köln am Rhein am 9. 10 und 11. September 1928* (Berlin: de Gruyter, 1928), pp. 141, 146–147.

49. Georg Solmssen, *Beiträge zur deutschen Politik und Wirtschaft, 1930–1933: Gesammelte Aufsätze und Vorträge* (Berlin: Duncker & Humblot, 1934), vol. 2, p. 250.

50. As described in Tilman Koops, ed., *Akten der Reichskanzlei, Weimarer Republik: Die Kabinette Brüning I und II,* vol. 2 (Boppard: Harald Boldt Verlag, 1982), p. 1332.

51. Hans Priester, *Das Geheimnis des 13. Juli: Ein Tatsachenbericht von der Bankenkrise* (Berlin: G. Stilke, 1932); Heinrich Brüning, *Memoiren, 1918–1934* (Stuttgart: Deutsche Verlags-Anstalt, 1970). For the subsequent interpretation of the crisis, see Gerald D. Feldman, "Jakob Goldschmidt, the History of the Banking Crisis of 1931, and the Problems of Freedom of Manoeuvre in the Weimar Republic," in Christoph Buchheim, Michael Hutter, and Harold James, eds., *Zerrissene Zwischenkriegszeit: Wirtschaftshistorische Beiträge; Knut Borchardt zum 65. Geburtstag* (Baden-Baden: Nomos, 1994), pp. 307–327.

52. Johannes Bähr and Dieter Ziegler, *Die Dresdner Bank*

in der Wirtschaft des Dritten Reichs (Munich: R. Oldenbourg, 2006), p. 82.

53. Schäffer diary entries, June 21, June 28, and July 5, 1932, ED93/21, Institut für Zeitgeschichte, Munich.

54. For the modern discussion, see Frank Rich, "The Ecstasy and the Agony," *New York Times,* March 1, 2009.

55. There is a fuller exposition of this argument in Harold James, *The End of Globalization: Lessons from the Great Depression* (Cambridge: Harvard University Press, 2001).

56. Quoted in Trevor Allen, *Ivar Kreuger: Match King Croesus and Crook* (London: John Long, 1932), pp. 230, 232.

57. Quoted in Ulf Olsson, *Marcus Wallenberg: Swedish Banker and Industrialist, 1899–1982* (Stockholm: Ekerlids, 2001), pp. 105-106.

58. As described in Hans Schäffer, "Marcus Wallenberg und die deutsche Bankenkrise 1931," manuscript ED93, March 5, 1939, p. 86, Institut für Zeitgeschichte, Munich.

59. This argument has been made most clearly by Charles Kindleberger in his *The World in Depression, 1929–1939* (Berkeley: University of California Press, 1973).

60. See Michael Bordo and Harold James, "Haberler versus Nurkse: The Case for Floating Exchange

Rates as an Alternative to Bretton Woods," in Arie Arnon and Warren Young, eds., *The Open Economy Macromodel: Past, Present, and Future* (Boston: Kluwer, 2002), pp. 161–182.

61. Barry Eichengreen and Ricardo Hausmann, "Exchange Rates and Financial Fragility," in Federal Reserve Bank of Kansas, *Proceedings* (1999): 329–361.

3. The Crash of 2008

1. George A. Akerlof and Robert J. Shiller, *Animal Spirits: How Human Psychology Drives the Economy, and Why It Matters for Global Capitalism* (Princeton, N.J.: Princeton University Press, 2009), p. 36; International Monetary Fund, *Global Financial Stability Report: Financial Distress and Deleveraging; Macro-Financial Implications and Policy* (Washington, D.C.: International Monetary Fund, October 2008).

2. See Roger Lowenstein, *When Genius Failed: The Rise and Fall of Long-Term Capital Management* (New York: Random House, 2000), pp. 185–214.

3. On the collapse, see William D. Cohan, *House of Cards: A Tale of Hubris and Wretched Excess on Wall Street* (New York: Doubleday, 2008).

4. Quoted in Martin Wolf, "The Rescue of Bear Stearns Marks Liberalisation's Limit," *Financial Times,* March 26, 2008, p. 13.

5. The Paul Volcker quotation can be viewed at http://

econclubny.org/files/Transcript_Volcker
_April_2008.pdf (accessed February 5, 2009).

6. Greenspan is quoted in the October 24, 2008,
edition of *Here Is the City;* see http://news
.hereisthecity.com/news/business_news/8386.cntns
(accessed February 5, 2009).

7. Quoted in Susanne Craig, Jeffrey McCracken,
Aaron Lucchetti, and Kate Kelly, "The Weekend
That Wall Street Died," *Wall Street Journal,* Decem-
ber 29, 2008, p. A1.

8. Ibid.

9. Jeffrey McCracken, "Lehman's Chaotic Bankruptcy
Filing Destroyed Billions in Value," *Wall Street Journal,* December 29, 2008, p. A10.

10. Quoted in Aline van Duyn, Deborah Brewster, and
Gillian Tett, "The Lehman Legacy," *Financial Times,*
October 13, 2008, p. 9.

11. John Gapper, "Take This Weekend Off, Hank," *Financial Times,* September 11, 2008.

12. Quoted in "The Week That Changed American
Capitalism," *Wall Street Journal,* September 20–21,
2008.

13. Quoted in Francesco Guerrera and Andrea Felsted,
"Inadequate Cover," *Financial Times,* October 7,
2008, p. 9.

14. See the quote at http://www.imf.org/External/AM/
2008/imfc/statement/eng/imf.pdf (accessed May 1,
2009).

15. "Brown's Misplaced Financial Patriotism," *Financial Times,* January 21, 2008, p. 10. See also John Gapper's blog at http://blogs.ft.com/gapperblog/2009/01/gordon-browns-misplaced-financial-patriotism (accessed February 5, 2009).

16. This argument was made most clearly in W. A. Lewis, *Economic Survey, 1919–1939* (1949; New York: Routledge, 2003).

17. This was the title of a famous article by John Maynard Keynes in *The Yale Review* 22, no. 4 (June 1933): 755–769.

18. E. E. Schattschneider, *Politics, Pressures, and the Tariff: A Study of Free Private Enterprise in Pressure Politics, as Shown in the 1929–1930 Revision of the Tariff* (New York: Prentice-Hall, 1935).

19. Tony Barber, "Jobless Migrants Should Leave, Say Many in the EU," *Financial Times,* March 16, 2009, p. 3. A full 54 percent in Britain oppose such migration, as opposed to 33 percent being in favor. The equivalent response in Germany is 49 and 43 percent, respectively.

20. See Christopher Jarvis, "The Rise and Fall of the Pyramid Schemes in Albania," International Monetary Fund working paper 99/98 (Washington, D.C.: IMF, 1999).

21. The classic text is Robert Keohane, *After Hegemony: Cooperation and Discord in the World Political Economy* (Princeton, N.J.: Princeton University Press, 1984).

22. Benn Steil and Robert E. Litan, *Financial Statecraft: The Role of Financial Markets in American Foreign Policy* (New Haven: Yale University Press, 2006), p. 132.

23. Peter B. Kenen, "Reform of the International Monetary Fund," Council on Foreign Relations, Council special report no. 29, May 2007, http://www.cfr.org/content/publications/attachments/IMF_CSR29.pdf (accessed April 22, 2009).

24. See Gianni Toniolo, with the assistance of Piet Clement, *Central Bank Cooperation at the Bank for International Settlements, 1930–1973* (Cambridge, Eng.: Cambridge University Press, 2005).

25. George Soros, *The Crisis of Global Capitalism: Open Society Endangered* (New York: Public Affairs, 1998), p. 102.

4. The Extent and Limit of the Financial Revolution

1. Frederic S. Mishkin, *The Next Great Globalization: How Disadvantaged Nations Can Harness Their Financial Systems to Get Rich* (Princeton, N.J.: Princeton University Press, 2006), p. 219.

2. Roman Frydman and Michael D. Goldberg, *Imperfect Knowledge Economics: Exchange Rates and Risk* (Princeton, N.J.: Princeton University Press, 2007), p. 295.

3. George Soros, *The New Paradigm for Financial Markets: The Credit Crisis of 2008 and What It Means* (New York: Public Affairs, 2008), p. 75.

4. See Rawi Abdelal, *Capital Rules: The Construction of Global Finance* (Cambridge: Harvard University Press, 2007).

5. The Turner Review: A Regulatory Response to the Global Financial Crisis, March 2009, http://www.fsa.gov.uk/pubs/other/turner_review.pdf (accessed April 22, 2009).

6. Ilse Mintz has shown how foreign bonds issued in New York deteriorated in the last years of the 1920s credit boom. See Ilse Mintz, *Deterioration in the Quality of Foreign Bonds Issued in the United States, 1920–1930* (New York: National Bureau of Economic Research, 1951).

7. International Monetary Fund, *Global Financial Stability Report* (Washington, D.C.: IMF, April 2008), chap. 1, p. 6.

8. Paul Samuelson, "Challenge to Judgment," *Journal of Portfolio Management* 1, no. 1 (1974): 17–19. See also Amar Bhidé, "In Praise of More Primitive Finance," Berkeley Electronic Press: Economists' Voice, February 2009, http://www.bhide.net/financial_crisis_2008/bhide_praise_of_primitive_finance.pdf (accessed April 22, 2009).

9. Gillian Tett, "The Dream Machine: The Invention of Credit Derivatives," *Financial Times Weekend Magazine,* March 24, 2006, p. 20.

10. Alan Greenspan, "The Structure of the International Financial System," Remarks at the Annual

Meeting of the Securities Industry Association, Boca Raton, Florida, November 5, 1998, http://www.federalreserve.gov/BoardDocs/Speeches/1998/19981105.htm (accessed April 22, 2009).

11. Gillian Tett, "Time Is Nigh to Put the True Value of CDOs Out in the Open," *Financial Times,* February 27, 2009, p. 22.

12. International Monetary Fund, Global Financial Stability Report, April 2008, p. 31, box 1.3; *Global Financial Stability Report* (Washington, D.C.: IMF, April 2009), chap. 3.

13. Francesco Guerrera, Nicole Bullock, and Julie Macintosh, "Wall Street Helped Banks' Demise," *Financial Times,* October 31, 2008, p. 17.

14. Blythe Masters is quoted in http://ncpainter.blogspot.com/2008/09/blythe-masters-in-her-own-words.html (accessed February 5, 2009).

15. Karl Marx and Friedrich Engels, *Selected Works* (London: Lawrence and Wishart, 1968), pp. 39, 51.

16. See Claudia Goldin and Lawrence F. Katz, *The Race between Education and Technology* (Cambridge: Belknap Press of Harvard University Press, 2008).

17. These figures are from B. R. Mitchell, *European Historical Statistics, 1750–1970* (London: Macmillan, 1975).

18. Quoted in Louise Armistead, "How HBOS Ran Out of Road," *Sunday Telegraph,* February 15, 2009, p. 5.

19. UBS, "Shareholder Report on UBS's Write-Downs," April 18, 2008, http://www.ubs.com/1/ShowMedia/

investors/shareholderreport?contentId=
140333&name=080418ShareholderReport.pdf (accessed April 22, 2009).

20. Quoted in Francesco Guerrera, Nicole Bullock, and
Julie Macintosh, "Iceland Asks Russia for $4 Bn. af-
ter West Refuses to Help," *Financial Times*, October
8, 2008, p. 4.

21. Mishkin, *Next Great Globalization*, p. 54.

22. See Luc Laeven and Fabian Valencia, "Systemic
Banking Crises: A New Database," International
Monetary Fund working paper WP/08/224 (Wash-
ington, D.C.: IMF, September 2008).

23. Gordon Brown, "We Will Put People First, Not
Bankers," *Observer* (London), February 22, 2009.

24. Quoted in Hans Schäffer diary, ED93/16, December
8, 1931, cabinet meeting, Institut für Zeitgeschichte,
Munich.

25. Bhidé, "In Praise of More Primitive Finance."

26. Quoted in David Pilling, "Japan Harks Back to an
Age of Innocence," *Financial Times*, March 5, 2009,
p. 15.

5. The Importance of Power Politics

1. Jeffry Frieden examines this issue in *Global Capitalism: Its Fall and Rise in the Twentieth Century* (New
York: W. W. Norton, 2006) without really providing
an explanation of why the correlations of democra-

tization or autocratization and economic crisis appear to be different in various historical eras.

2. Kindleberger makes the point most explicitly in *The World in Depression* (Berkeley: University of California Press, 1973).

3. Peer Steinbrück quoted in David Leonhardt, "A Power That May Not Stay So Super," *New York Times Weekend,* October 12, 2008, p. 1.

4. National Intelligence Council, *Global Trends, 2025: A Transformed World* (Washington, D.C.: NIC, 2008), p. 8.

5. Quoted in John Thornhill, Quentin Peel, and Charles Clover, "Sarkozy Welcomes Russia Plan for Security," *Financial Times,* October 9, 2008, p. 8.

6. Melchior Palyi, "Bares Shaken Faith Abroad in U.S. Dollar," *Tribune* (Chicago), September 17, 1950.

7. Thomas Balogh, *The Dollar Crisis: Causes and Cure* (Oxford, Eng.: Basil Blackwell, 1949); Jacques Rueff, *Balance of Payments: Proposals for the Resolution of the Most Pressing World Economic Problem of Our Time* (New York: Macmillan, 1967); Egon Sohmen, *Flexible Exchange Rates* (Chicago: Chicago University Press, 1969).

8. Robert Triffin, *Gold and the Dollar Crisis: The Future of Convertibility* (New Haven: Yale University Press, 1960).

9. Michael P. Dooley, David Folkerts-Landau, and Pe-

ter Garber, "An Essay on the Revived Bretton Woods System," National Bureau of Economic Research working paper no. 9971 (Washington, D.C.: NBER, September 2003). For a survey of the debate, see Paul Wachtel, "Understanding the Old and New Bretton Woods," paper presented at the conference In Search of a New Bretton Woods: Reserve Currencies and Global Imbalances, Florence, October 20, 2006. Barry Eichengreen gives a more skeptical view without succumbing to undue alarmism in *Global Imbalances and the Lessons of Bretton Woods* (Cambridge: MIT Press, 2006).

10. Harold James, *International Monetary Cooperation since Bretton Woods* (New York: Oxford University Press, 1996).

11. Robert Triffin, "Discussion," in Francesco Giavazzi, Stefano Micossi, and Marcus Miller, eds., *The European Monetary System* (Cambridge, Eng.: Cambridge University Press, 1988), pp. 41–43; Robert Z. Lawrence, "Rude Awakening: The End of the American Dream," *International Economic Insights* 1, no. 1 (January–February 1994): 2–6.

12. IMF figures from *Annual Reports;* see http://www.imf.org/external/pubs/ft/ar/index.htm. See also Philip D. Wooldridge, "The Changing Composition of Official Reserves," *BIS Quarterly Review* (September 2006).

13. "China's Government Is Top Foreign Holder," *Wall Street Journal*, July 11, 2008; Olga Varilyeva, "Volume of Russia's Investments in U.S. Mortgage Banks Shrinks," *Russian Corporate World* 3, no. 9 (October 2008).

14. This was a point made very effectively by Tim Congdon: see Lombard Street Research Ltd., "The Analyses of Unsustainability, and Total Unsustainability, Based on the Familiar Theory of Debt Dynamics Have Been Dumbfounded," *Monthly Economic Review* (November–December 2002): 5. For a fuller analysis, see Pierre-Olivier Gourinchas and Hélène Rey, "From World Banker to World Venture Capitalist: U.S. External Adjustment and the Exorbitant Privilege," National Bureau of Economic Research working paper no. 11563 (Washington, D.C.: NBER, August 2005), as well as Ricardo Caballero, Emmanuel Farhi, and Pierre-Olivier Gourinchas, "An Equilibrium Model of Global Imbalances and Low Interest Rates," National Bureau of Economic Research working paper no. 11996 (Washington, D.C.: NBER, 2006). Ricardo Haussmann and Federico Sturzenegger, in their "Global Imbalances or Bad Accounting? The Missing Dark Matter in the Wealth of Nations," Harvard Center for International Development working paper 124 (Cambridge: Harvard Center for

International Development, January 2006), make a slightly different case for longer-term sustainability based on invisible exports and assets.

15. Alessandra Fogli and Fabrizio Perri, "The 'Great Moderation' of the U.S. External Imbalance," European University Institute working paper (Florence: EUI, March 2007).

16. Bureau of Economic Analysis, National Income: Table 2.1, Personal Income and Its Disposition, http://www.bea.gov/national/nipaweb (accessed April 30, 2009).

17. Though see Keith Bradsher, *High and Mighty SUVs: The World's Most Dangerous Vehicles and How They Got That Way* (New York: Public Affairs, 2002).

18. See Paco Underhill, *Call of the Mall* (New York: Simon & Schuster, 2004).

19. A good survey is Isaac Ehrlich, "The Mystery of Human Capital as Engine of Growth; or, Why the U.S. Became the Economic Superpower in the Twentieth Century," National Bureau of Economic Research working paper no. 12868 (Washington, D.C.: NBER, January 2007).

20. Joseph S. Nye, *Soft Power: The Means to Success in World Politics* (New York: Public Affairs, 2004).

21. See Adrian Favell, *Eurostars and Eurocities: Free Movement and Mobility in an Integrating Europe* (Oxford, Eng.: Blackwell, 2008).

22. Emile Despres, Charles P. Kindleberger, and Walter

S. Salant, "The Dollar and World Liquidity: A Minority View," *Economist* (February 11, 1966).

23. President of the United States, *The National Security Strategy of the United States of America*, September 2002.

24. Quoted in Alain Peyrefitte, *C'était de Gaulle* (Paris: Galliard, 2003), p. 664. See also Francis J. Gavin, *Gold, Dollars, and Power: The Politics of International Monetary Relations, 1958–1968* (Chapel Hill: University of North Carolina Press, 2004), p. 121.

25. Lawrence Kotlikoff and Niall Ferguson, "Going Critical," *National Interest* (Fall 2003).

26. See J. H. Elliott, *Empires of the Atlantic World: Britain and Spain in America, 1492–1830* (New Haven: Yale University Press, 2006).

27. Adam Smith, *The Wealth of Nations* (Chicago: University of Chicago Press, 1976), vol. 5, chap. 3, pp. 446, 466–467.

28. In 1970, Robert Mundell reached a similar conclusion: see Alexandre Swoboda, ed., *L'Union monétaire en Europe* (Geneva: HEI, 1971).

29. Barry Eichengreen, "The Euro as a Reserve Currency," *Journal of the Japanese and International Economies* 12 (1998): 483–506; Marcello de Cecco, "From Monopoly to Oligopoly: Lessons from the Pre-1914 Experience," in Eric Helleiner and Jonathan Kirshner, eds., *The Future of the Dollar* (Ithaca: Cornell University Press, 2009). See also Gabriele Galati

and Philip D. Wooldridge, "The Euro as a Reserve Currency: A Challenge to the Pre-eminence of the U.S. Dollar?" Bank for International Settlements working paper no. 218 (Basel: BIS, October 2006).

30. Eichengreen, *Global Imbalances*, p. 26; Dooley, Folkerts-Landau, and Garber, "An Essay on the Revived Bretton Woods System."

31. Lorenzo Bini Smaghi, "Financial Crisis: Where Does Europe Stand?" speech made in Brussels, February 12, 2009, http://www.ecb.int/press/key/date/2009/html/sp090212.en.html (accessed March 12, 2009).

32. David Marsh, *The Euro* (New Haven: Yale University Press, 2009).

33. John Burton and Anuj Gangahar, "Temasek in $4.4 bn. Merrill Vote," *Financial Times,* December 27, 2007, p. 14.

34. Martin Wolf, *Fixing Global Finance* (Baltimore: Johns Hopkins University Press, 2008), p. 192.

35. See the discussion of what he terms "Chimerica" in Niall Ferguson, *The Ascent of Money: A Financial History of the World* (London: Penguin, 2008), pp. 333–340.

36. Yasheng Huan, *Capitalism with Chinese Characteristics: Entrepreneurship and the State* (Cambridge, Eng.: Cambridge University Press, 2008), p. 212.

37. See the arguments of John Gerard Ruggie in his *Winning the Peace: America and World Order in the New*

Era (New York: Columbia University Press, 1996); and G. John Ikenberry, *After Victory: Institutions, Strategic Restraint, and the Rebuilding of Order after Major Wars* (Princeton, N.J.: Princeton University Press, 2001).

6. Uncertainty of Values

1. See Benjamin Friedman, *The Moral Consequences of Economic Growth* (New York: Knopf, 2005).
2. G-20 Summit, Leaders' Statement, April 2, 2009, http://www.g20.org/Documents/ g20_communique_020409.pdf (accessed April 25, 2009).
3. Sophocles, *The Theban Plays,* trans. E. F. Watling (Harmondsworth, Eng.: Penguin, 1947), p. 26.
4. Benn Steil and Robert E. Litan, *Financial Statecraft: The Role of Financial Markets in American Foreign Policy* (New Haven: Yale University Press, 2006), p. 165. See also similar arguments in Benn Steil and Manuel Hinds, *Money, Markets, and Sovereignty* (New Haven: Yale University Press, 2009).
5. Karl Helfferich, *Das Geld* (Leipzig: C. L. Hirschfeld, 1903), pp. 528, 530.
6. Elias Canetti, *Die Fackel im Ohr: Lebensgeschichte, 1921–1931* (Munich: C. Hanser, 1993); Gerald D. Feldman, *The Great Disorder: Politics, Economics, and Society in the German Inflation, 1914–1924* (New York: Oxford University Press, 1993).

7. Ben Bernanke, Thomas Laubach, Frederic Mishkin, and Adam Posen, *Inflation Targeting: Lessons from the International Experience* (Princeton, N.J.: Princeton University Press, 1999), p. 322.

8. Remarks by Governor Ben S. Bernanke at the Annual Washington Policy Conference of the National Association of Business Economists, Washington, D.C., March 25, 2003, http://www.federalreserve.gov/Boarddocs/Speeches/2003/20030325/default.htm (accessed April 22, 2009).

9. Frederic Mishkin and Eugene White, "U.S. Stock Market Crashes and Their Aftermath: Implications for Monetary Policy," National Bureau of Economic Research working paper no. 8992 (Washington, D.C.: NBER, June 2002).

10. Schacht in 1925, from Federal Reserve Bank of New York, Benjamin Strong Papers, quoted in Harold James, *The Reichsbank and Public Finance in Germany, 1924–1933* (Frankfurt: Fritz Knapp, 1985), p. 29.

11. Otmar Issing, *The Birth of the Euro,* trans. Nigel Hulbert (Cambridge, Eng.: Cambridge University Press, 2008).

12. See, for instance, Barry Eichengreen in his *Golden Fetters: The Gold Standard and the Great Depression, 1919–1939* (New York: Oxford University Press, 1992), p. 198: "The second half of the 1920s was marked by steady deflation."

13. Melchior Palyi, *The Twilight of Gold, 1914–1936* (Chicago: Regnery, 1972).

14. Lionel Robbins, *The Great Depression* (London: Macmillan, 1934), p. 48.

15. John Maynard Keynes, *A Treatise on Money* (London: Macmillan, 1930), vol. 2, p. 190.

16. Robert Skidelsky, *John Maynard Keynes: A Biography,* vol. 2: *The Economist as Saviour, 1920–1937* (London: Macmillan, 1992), p. 318.

17. See, for instance, Murray Rothbard, *America's Great Depression* (Princeton, N.J.: Van Nostrand, 1963).

18. Interview with Hirst by Angus Watson, *Financial Times,* October 11, 2008, p. 24.

19. Jonathan K. Nelson and Richard J. Zeckhauser, *The Patron's Payoff: Conspicuous Commissions in Italian Renaissance Art* (Princeton, N.J.: Princeton University Press, 2008).

20. Deutsche Bank, db-artmag.de, 05 (2002–2003), quoting speech of Dr. Tessen von Heydebreck, November 13, 2002, http://www.db-artmag.de/05/e/thema-ankaeufe-heydebreck.php (accessed April 25, 2009); Kjell Nordström and Jonas Ridderbrake, *Funky Business: Talent Makes Capital Dance* (Harlow, Eng.: Pearson, 2000), p. 158.

21. George Soros, *The New Paradigm for Financial Markets: The Credit Crisis of 2008 and What It Means* (New York: Public Affairs, 2008), p. 38.

22. Remarks by Governor Ben S. Bernanke before the National Economists Club, Washington, D.C., November 21, 2002, "Deflation: Making Sure 'It' Doesn't Happen Here," http://www.federalreserve.gov/boardDocs/speeches/2002/20021121/default.htm (accessed April 22, 2009).

23. Bank for International Settlements, *76th Annual Report, 2006* (Basel: BIS, 2006), p. 141.

24. Roger Bootle, *The Death of Inflation: Surviving and Thriving in the Zero Era* (London: Roger Brealey, 1998).

25. Claudio Borio and Andrew Filardo, "Looking Back at the International Deflation Record," *North American Journal of Economics and Finance* 15 (2004): 287–311; Michael Bordo and Andrew Filardo, "Deflation and Monetary Policy in a Historical Perspective: Remembering the Past or Being Condemned to Repeat It?" *Economic Policy* 20 (2005): 799–844.

26. Gustav Stolper in *Der deutsche Volkswirt,* quoted in Toni Stolper, *Gustav Stolper: Ein Leben in Brennpunkten unserer Zeit; Wien, Berlin, New York* (Tübingen: R. Wunderlich, 1960), p. 287.

27. Charles Bean, quoted in *Daily Mail* (London), October 25, 2009, http://www.dailymail.co.uk/news/article-1080172/Worst-financial-crisis-human-history-Bank-boss-warning-pound-suffers-biggest-fall-37-years.html (accessed April 25, 2009).

28. Irving Fisher, "The Debt-Deflation Theory of Great Depressions," *Econometrica* 1, no. 3 (1933): 227–357.

29. Henry Paulson remarks, December 11, 2008, http://www.treasury.gov/press/releases/hp1301.htm (accessed March 1, 2009).

30. Quoted in John Authers and Gillian Tett, "Ins and Outs of the Ups and Downs," *Financial Times,* January 25, 2008, p. 8; see also Stanley Fish, "Faith and Deficits," *New York Times,* March 1, 2009, http://fish.blogs.nytimes.com/2009/03/01/faith-and-deficits/?scp=1&sq=faith%20and%20deficits%20fish&st=cse (accessed April 22, 2009); James Kirkup, "Financial Markets Need Morality, Gordon Brown Tells Labour Conference," *Daily Telegraph* (London), March 7, 2009, p. 10.

31. See Amar Bhidé, "In Praise of More Primitive Finance," Berkeley Electronic Press: Economists' Voice, February 2009, http://www.bhide.net/financial_crisis_2008/bhide_praise_of_primitive_finance.pdf (accessed April 30, 2009).

32. See the 1980 encyclical of John Paul II, *Dives in misericordia:* "The present-day mentality, more perhaps than that of people in the past, seems opposed to a God of mercy and in fact tends to exclude from life and to remove from the human heart the very idea of mercy. The word and the concept of 'mercy' seem to cause uneasiness in man,

who, thanks to the enormous development of science and technology never before known in history, has become the master of the earth and has subdued and dominated it. This dominion over the earth, sometimes understood in a one-sided and superficial way, seems to leave no room for mercy." See http://www.vatican.va/holy_father/ john_paul_ii/encyclicals/documents/hf_jp-ii_ enc_30111980_dives-in-misericordia_en.html (accessed April 30, 2009).

33. George Soros, *The Crisis of Global Capitalism: Open Society Endangered* (New York: Public Affairs, 1998), p. 197.

34. Barack Obama, Inaugural Address, January 20, 2009, http://www.nytimes.com/2009/01/20/us/ politics/20text-obama.html (accessed April 22, 2009).

35. Zhou Xiaochuan, "On Savings Ratio," March 24, 2009, http://www.pbc.gov.cn/English (accessed April 22, 2009).

36. On the influence of business schools, see Rakesh Khurana, *From Higher Aims to Hired Hands: The Social Transformation of American Business Schools and the Unfulfilled Promise of Management as a Profession* (Princeton, N.J.: Princeton University Press, 2007).

37. Steven Shapin, *The Scientific Life: A Moral History of a Late Modern Vocation* (Chicago: University of Chicago Press, 2008).

INDEX